CU01456871

INTERWOVEN STRANDS

1660-1947

A History of a Country Town and the Role
of Solicitors in developing its Institutions

by
Peter Criddle

First Published in Great Britain in 2006 by Tucann Books
Text & Images © Peter Criddle All rights reserved
Design © TUCANN*design&print*

No part of this publication may be reproduced or transmitted in any way or by
any means, including electronic storage and retrieval, without prior permission
of the publisher.

ISBN 10: 1 873257 72 4
ISBN 13: 9781873257722

Produced by: TUCANN*design&print*, 19 High Street, Heighington Lincoln LN4 1RG
Tel & Fax: 01522 790009
www.tucann.co.uk

CONTENTS

INTRODUCTION

Rather more than half a century ago, a country solicitor, Reginald Hine, wrote in his Confessions of an Uncommon Attorney of the career of 40 years he had had practising in what he then described as 'the little town of Hitchin in Hertfordshire' in a very old firm which happily still flourishes there. He was Uncommon as a solicitor, he said, because he had enjoyed his work so much. The profession was not what it was and the modern solicitors of 1945, he thought, no longer enjoyed their jobs in that "pestering post-war age".

Reginald Hine's book touched upon the history of his famous firm but it largely consisted of personal reminiscences by no means confined to his experiences as a country solicitor. He was, however, devoted to Hitchin and, insofar as he was chronicling life in the town, he felt himself to be producing a little mirror of the world 'for the story of an English town is the history of England itself'.

Hitchin is no longer a little country town. But in a small market town like Alford in Lincolnshire, a county rather off the beaten track, it has still been possible for one to have enjoyed nearly 40 years of practice as a country solicitor in much the same way as Hine did. And twenty-first century Alford can still represent a mirror of that English life which has so often elsewhere disappeared.

As was traditionally the case in English country towns, the history of solicitors in Alford was closely intertwined with the history of the town itself. Right up until at least the Second World War central government had little to do with the management of local affairs. Perhaps until the eighteenth century they were indeed largely unmanaged. But gradually communications improved, the countryside was developed, local industries appeared, financial facilities were regularised and the Law itself, with the multiplying of statutory provisions, ceased to be concerned in general merely with the settling of disputes between one citizen and another. In the absence of civil servants, local government officials, educational administrators, stipendiary court officers or even, until relatively late times, country bankers, it was country solicitors who were on hand to fulfil these roles. Perhaps the climax of their influence was in the mid-nineteenth century. The local history of Alford represents in microcosm what was happening across the English countryside and the records of an old-established legal practice there can perhaps help to bring to life the story of the little town and also possibly provide an illustration of how the profession of a country solicitor has developed and changed over a period of three or four centuries.

PART ONE

CONTINUITY AND CHANGE

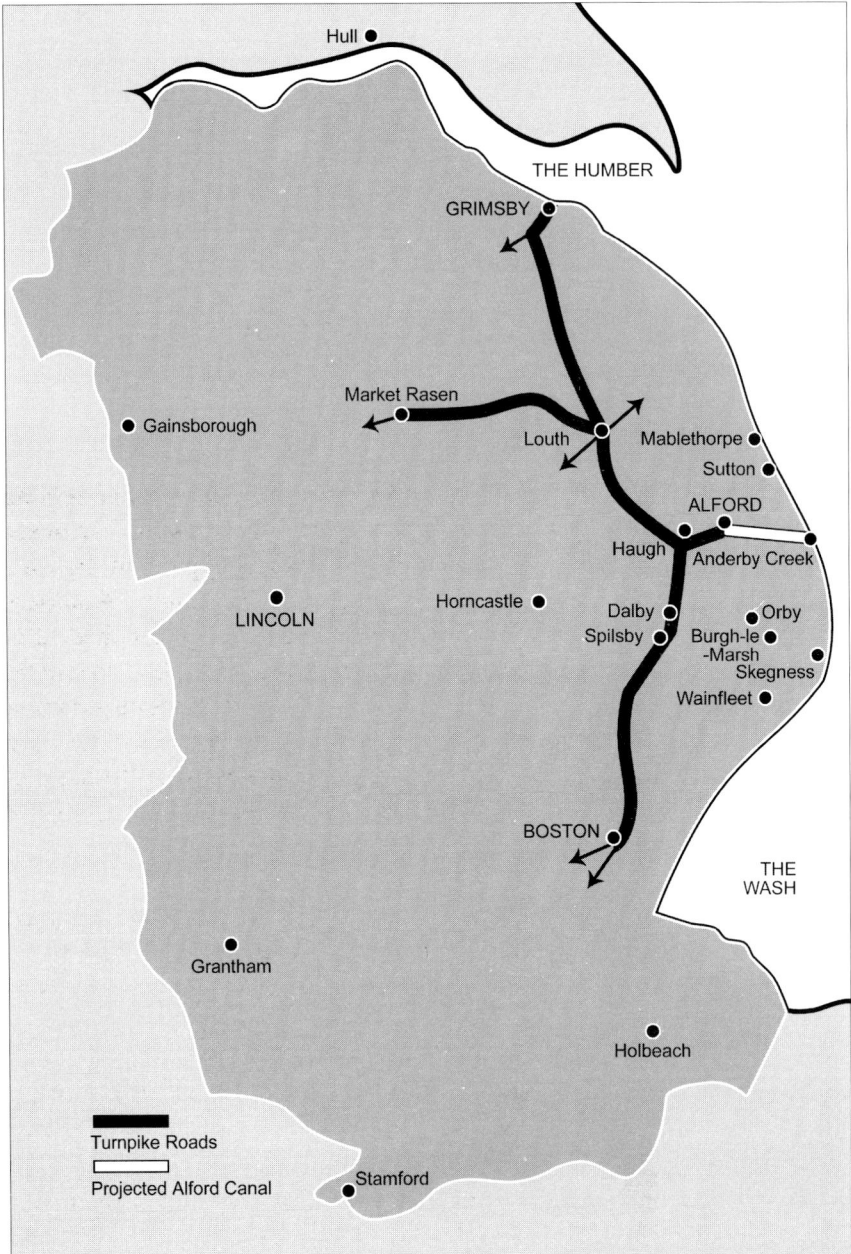

1. Alford's situation in Lincolnshire in relation to 18th century Turnpike Roads

CHAPTER ONE

The Lawyers of Seventeenth and Eighteenth Century Alford

From very early times in England, there had been complaints as to the numbers and rapacity of lawyers. They were variously described as vultures, vipers, locusts or 'grasshoppers of Egypt'. The diarist John Evelyn in 1700 noted 'the Exorbitant Numbers of Attourneys now indeede swarming and evidently causing suits and disturbance by eating out the Estate of people'. And idealistic clergymen such as Robert Sanderson, for 40 years a country parson before becoming Bishop of Lincoln in 1660, set up machinery for the settling of differences on Christian principles in order to prevent parishioners falling into the hands of the rapacious lawyers of the time.

During the sixteenth and seventeenth centuries barristers had managed to regulate themselves as largely a separate profession. But, despite several attempts, Parliament had been unable to curb the numbers of what had become regarded as the lower branch of the legal profession. Yet half the attorneys or solicitors probably practised in London and most of the remainder in other cities or large towns with the result that supply in very small country towns did not perhaps generally exceed demand. Of attorneys recognised as such in London, there were recorded as being only 4 in the whole of Lincolnshire in 1588. The county was, in any case, at this time very isolated and impoverished and in the early seventeenth century was subjected to widespread outbreaks of plague. So small a town as Alford suffered 94 deaths from the plague there in 1630 and afterwards the area was struck by famine. Economic conditions locally improved, however,

2. A Seventeenth Century Lawyer

3. Alford's major 17th century landowner, Sir Robert Christopher

as the century progressed and the numbers of solicitors greatly increased. By 1660 William Willerton was already established as a prominent citizen in the town. In those days the Governors of the Grammar School were the most influential body of townspeople and William Willerton was one.

Not only was the growth in the numbers of solicitors a problem in itself but solicitors as a body were under no real sort of discipline or control and many of them had little or no qualification or training for practising in the law. In country areas such as East Lincolnshire, however, seventeenth century solicitors, rather than having had formal legal training, often seem to have started their careers working in a clerical capacity for local landowners and then to have graduated to a position of land agent or

4. Sir Robert Christopher's Alford Manor House

general man of business, together with appointment as steward to one or more of the local manorial courts. One such seems to have been William Hardy. In the Will of the Alford magnate, Sir Robert Christopher, proved in 1670, he is mentioned as one of a number of men given 20 shillings each for rings 'who have been related to me as clerks' and Vaughan Bonner, a successor as Alford solicitor, appears to have started by gaining practical experience working for local landowners in much the same way. Eventually deeds describe both Hardy and Bonner as 'Gentlemen', a title to which attorneys could not always aspire.

5. Alford Solicitors included in an early Law List

Mr Gonville London 3rd April 1744

Sir

I received yours of the 31st ulto which I communicated to my Lady Dutchess, who has signed the Power of Attorney for your keeping Her Graces Courts, which I here enclose you. Her Grace commands me to give you her service and does not doubt but you will fullfill your promise in endeavouring to the utmost of your power to regulate Her Courts & put the Rolls in good order, if Mr Abbot has not transcribed the Rolls since Mr Bonner's time into the Court Book which was sent him with the Rolls for that purpose, Her Grace desires you will do them as soon as time will permit. I hope Mr Headon will take care to get the books and all the Rolls and papers that relate to her Grace in due time from Mr Abbot's Executor, that you may be inabled to hold both courts at the propper time, I beg my humble service to Mrs Gonville & am Sir

Your most humble servant
J Patten

PS Lord Robert & Lord Charles set out for fflanders this morning. I made your compliments as you desired.

6. Letter from the Duchess of Rutland's London Agent in 1744 confirming William Gonville's appointment as her Court Steward in succession to Samuel Abbott and Vaughan Bonner. Illustration No 92 on page 121 suggests the link-up through Bonner with the seventeenth century practice of William Willerton.

Vera Effigies Viri
Equitis aurati nuper
ad Placita coram

clariſs EDOARDI COKE
Capitalis Iuſticiári
Rege tenenda aſsignat

R. White ſculp

7. Sir Edward Coke who has been called "the greatest of English lawyers"

Comprehensive Law Lists detailing solicitors did not appear until 1775 but local manorial court records are helpful in tracing the solicitors practising in Alford before that time. Vaughan Bonner and his predecessors William and John Hardy held several such stewardships and in the mid-eighteenth century Samuel Abbott, William Gonville and Thomas Marwood successively followed. The Alford of those days, with a population of only 500 or so, can hardly have supported substantial solicitors' practices in

Lib. 2.   Of Homage.   Sect. 87

Sect. 87.

Pur ceo que n'eſt convenient, &c. By this it appeareth, [m] that *argumentum ab inconvenienti plurimùm valet in lege,* as often ſhall be obſerved hereafter. *Non ſolum quod licet ſed quid eſt convenient eſt conſiderandum. Nihil quod eſt inconveniens, eſt licitum* (1).

ITEM ſi feme ſole ferra homage a ſon ſeignior, el ne dirra, Jeo deveigne voſtre feme ; pur ceo que n'eſt convenient que feme dirra, que il deviendra feme a aſcun home, forſque a ſa baron, quant el eſt eſpouſe. Mes el dirra, Jeo face a vous homage, et a vous ſerra foial et loial, et foy a vous portera des tenements que jeo teigne de vous, ſalve la foy que jeo doy a noſtre ſeignior le roy.

ALSO if a woman ſole ſhall doe homage, ſhe ſhal not ſay, I become your woman; for it is not fitting that a woman ſhould ſay that ſhe will become a woman to any man, but to her huſband, when ſhe is married. But ſhe ſhall ſay, I do to you homage, and to you ſhall be faithfull and true, and faith to you ſhall bear for the tenements I hold of you, ſaving the faith I owe to our ſoveraigne lord the king.

8. "Coke upon Littleton" the standard legal textbook for a couple of centuries after its publication in 1628; the text is written in law-French and English side-by-side

competition with each other and it seems likely that the stewardships were, as was commonly the case, generally handed down from principal to principal in the continuing legal practice. And, when the early Law Lists appeared, John Elye (who practised at Alford around 1759-1780) is mentioned along with William Carnley, who had sometimes deputised for Elye as Orby Manorial Court steward before taking over the stewardship himself.

In the course of the eighteenth century the standing of solicitors very much improved. An Act of Parliament of 1729 began the process of regulation. Before admission to the Rolls, a prospective solicitor had to be apprenticed for five years under Articles of Clerkship in a solicitor's office and to undergo examination by a judge. The examination was only informal but it nevertheless seems to have concentrated the mind upon the knowledge of the law required. William Hickey in his Memoirs describes being 'in a terrible fright' about the ordeal he imagined he had to pass through, although in fact the examining judge was an old friend of his father's, who, after a few pleasantries over the breakfast table, took him over to court by coach for the admission ceremonial. A well-used copy of Coke upon Littleton, the standard student text book of those days, can still be seen at what was once William Carnley's office in Alford and the eighteenth century law student was not really expected to go much beyond this. But Carnley was well qualified academically as a Bachelor of Laws and detailed notes in old books of law reports and statutes show that he kept himself up to date.

By 1800 country solicitors were involved in work of many kinds. Rural areas such as Lincolnshire were being opened up by the creation of turnpike roads and the landscape was being further developed by enclosures of common land and improvements in land drainage. All these made work for solicitors whether in negotiating and piloting through the necessary parliamentary Acts or in the subsequent increased conveyancing. Manorial court stewardships remained important. Several of these were operated by William Carnley for local Lords of the Manor and he was still typical of country solicitors in continuing in his double capacity of local solicitor and Land Agent for the Manners Estate which owned most of the land in the Alford area. Towards the end of the eighteenth century William Carnley was further involved in law enforcement both in the administration of

10. The High Street office premises, a view little changed since William Carnley put on the new frontage in 1801

the newly-established local Court of Requests and as secretary of the Alford Association for the Prosecution of Felons. And, in the absence of country banking facilities, local solicitors such as William Carnley were, as Money Scriveners, the people to approach for clients with money to invest in loans and by those wishing to take money up on mortgage.

Altogether eighteenth century country lawyers had become substantial figures in their local communities with incomes that have been estimated at as much as £250-£300 a year. Most of them had traditionally been peripatetic, visiting clients in their homes and doing the paperwork in their own houses with only perhaps an articled clerk boarding with them to help with their labours. But many by the turn of the century were acquiring substantial town-centre buildings, part of which, though still generally only a small part, would be used as office premises for receiving clients. Such buildings were among the most prominent in country towns and many with their Georgian frontages still survive. The one purchased by William Carnley in 1801 is still occupied by his successors today. But Carnley's practice

LINCOLNSHIRE.

TO BE

SOLD BY AUCTION,

(UNLESS BEFORE DISPOSED OF, BY PRIVATE CONTRACT.)

At the *Blue Stone Inn*, in Louth, in the said County, on *Wednesday* the 2d. day of October next, between the Hours of 3 and 6 o'Clock in the afternoon, in the following Lots; subject to such Conditions of Sale, as will be then and there produced; The following VALUABLE

Freehold Estates,

Situate in the Parishes of *North Somercotes*, *Saltfleetby*, and *Sailby*, in the County of Lincoln.

In North Somercotes, by admeasurement (more or less)

		A. R. P.	A. R. P.
Lot 1.	A piece of Land intermixed with Lands of Mr. Scrope, in a Close called 2½ *Acres*, by the Eau Bank, in Tenure of Peter Hagworthingham. — — —	}	0 2 0
Lot 2.	A Close of rich Meadow or Pasture Ground, in 4 Divisions, on the South Side of the Eau Bank, in tenure of Mr. S. Caley. — — —	}	17 2 0
Lot 3.	A piece of Meadow Land, intermixed with Lands of Lord Yarborough, in a Close called 19 *Acres*, in tenure of Mr. Blinkhorn. — — — —	}	2 0 0

In Saltfleetby, in tenure of Robert Webster.

Lot 4.	A Close of rich Pasture Land, called the Ten *Acres*.	7 2 15	
	Ditto— — — — — — — the Seven *Acres*.	7 2 36 } 23 2 6	
	Ditto— — — — — — — the Eleven *Acres*.	8 0 35	

N. B. *This Lot is subject to a quit-rent of 1s. 8l. payable to Magdalen College Oxford.*

In tenure of Thomas Webster.

Lot 5.	A Cottage & Garden, with a Common right on the Banks.		
	The Homestead, rich Pasture, — — — —	1 0 20	
	Gares, — — — — — — — — —	3 2 14	
	Stewton Stripes, First — — — — — —	1 0 50 } 8 1 22	
	Second Meadow — — — — —	1 1 18	
	Third — — — — — —	0 3 30	
	Fourth — — — — — —	0 0 20	

In Sailby, in tenure of John Clarke,

Lot 6.	A Close of rich Pasture Land, called the Homestead.	2 1 15	
	Ditto — — — — — — the Spring Close.	1 3 4	
	Several pieces of Arable & Meadow Land in the East field	12 3 16 } 21 0 1	
	Ditto — — — — — in Thoresthorpe field	4 0 6	

In tenure of John Parnill

Lot 7	A Cottage and Homestead — — — —	2 0 33	
	Arable and Meadow, in the East field, — — —	2 2 17 } 4 3 10	

☞ The several Tenants will shew the Premises, and further Particulars may be known at *Mr. Carnley's Office,* ALFORD.

26th. August, 1799.

C. STAINBAN ☐☐☐☐ BOOKBINDER and BOOKSELLER, BOSTON.

9. Sale notice of 1799 showing that William Carnley was an early lawyer to operate from office premises

was clearly by then a well-established one as early property sales advertising shows he had already for some time been operating from tenanted office premises in the town.

William Carnley's move to the new High Street premises and the construction there of the imposing new facade on what appears previously to have been a simpler thatched building seems to have been part of optimistic plans for the future. He was 55 and was apparently keen that his 12-year-old son, also William, should eventually join him in the practice. Carnley was, however, an elderly father. In 1805 he fell ill and had to take a young partner, Titus Bourne, to continue the practice. His firm continued for about a year as Carnley and Bourne but in 1806 William Carnley died.

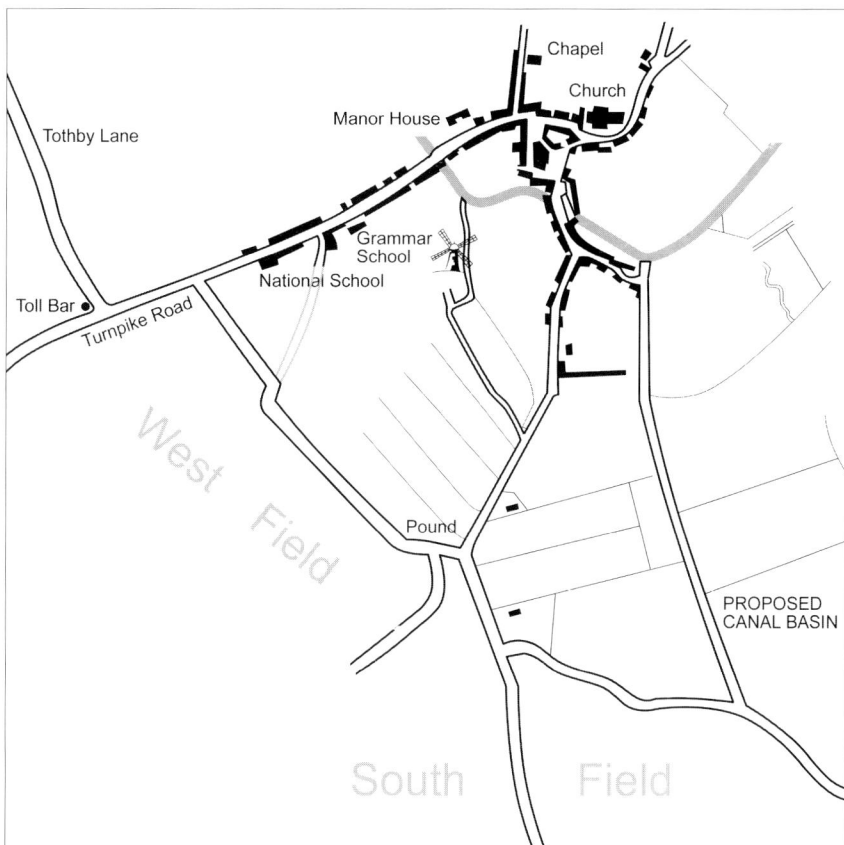

11. Alford in 1825 showing the Common Fields (see p63) and the Turnpike Road (see p79) and the proposed canal terminal (see p82)

CHAPTER TWO

Titus Bourne 1805-1859
in the Age of Improvement

For families such as the Bournes of Dalby the early eighteenth century was a time of very great prosperity. They and other local families like them such as the Franklins, the Brackenburys, the Tennysons, and the Sellwoods had been doing very well out of the economic development of the countryside over the past half century or so. Such families were closely interconnected either by marriage or in business ventures as lawyers, land agents or bankers. And it was these professional connections as much as their property holdings which gave this handful of East Lincolnshire families their exceptional authority in local affairs.

12. Alford in the time of Titus Bourne

13. Dalby Hall.
The building burnt
down in 1841

Dalby Hall had been in the Bourne family since 1720. The current John Bourne, who had married a Tennyson, lived there and his younger brother George, Titus Bourne's father, lived at Haugh a few miles out of Alford. George Bourne had had a distinguished career. He had been a page at the Royal Court and as a young man had been sent over on a mission to Germany to bring home 17-year-old Princess Charlotte Sophia of Mecklenburg-Strelitz as King George III's bride. After a spell in the army as a Lieutenant in the 5th Dragoon Guards, he had settled down at Haugh and, as a respected sheep farmer, was referred to by the noted agriculturalist Arthur Young in his General Review of the Agriculture of Lincolnshire. He was for some time a land agent, another traditional Bourne family occupation, and he also took part in the bank which the Franklin and Bourne families ran together from Spilsby, Alford and Horncastle. In January 1811, the Gentleman's Magazine announced his death: "At the moment he had stepped into his gig to take his daily airing, George Bourne Esq., of Haugh near Spilsby".

The Bourne family withdrew from the Franklin, Bourne and Franklin banking partnership in 1805 and some time afterwards the Franklin Bank, which continued at Spilsby, was one of a number of Lincolnshire private banks of the time which failed. Titus Bourne, George Bourne's second son, born in 1783, had first been introduced to banking by the family firm but older Bourne relatives had been solicitors in Louth. And in 1805 he was ready to move to Alford to work in partnership with William Carnley, then in the decline of life, with a view to taking over his legal practice.

Right up until almost the end of old William Carnley's time, there does not seem to have been any competing practice in the town. But the early nineteenth century was the so-called Age of Improvement. Lincolnshire was further opened up, first by canals and then by the railways which came to Alford in 1848. Agriculture for farmers, and so indirectly for shopkeepers and professional people, was prosperous. The Napoleonic Wars had ensured high prices for agricultural produce and, after a brief post-war slump, high prices for home-grown wheat returned as a result of trade protection under the Corn Laws. The great re-building, which had happened much earlier in the South of England, now took place in Lincolnshire. Substantial brick-built farmhouses and cottages sprang up all over the county and re-building radically improved the appearance of the towns. Altogether these were for Lincolnshire solicitors their halcyon days. Several new practices opened up in Alford, including a substantial one, Wilson & Portington, which operated for many years from the handsome house facing the parish church. The very old-established Spilsby firm, Walker & Co, opened a branch office in the town. And Titus Bourne for his part had a branch office at Spilsby which he attended on the Monday market days.

14. Hanby Hall: This Georgian house in the early nineteenth century belonged to lawyers and the firm of Wilson and Portington operated from the annexed legal office shown on the left of the picture.

If, however, the Age of Improvement was a fortunate time for the landed gentry and for prosperous businesspeople, it was certainly not so for many poor people in country areas. Corn Law protection did not benefit them and, like the urban poor, they suffered badly from the high cost of bread. And George Robinson, who practised in a modest way in Alford from 1819 to 1859, was known as "the Poor Man's Lawyer" because he was never known to advise his clients to go to law if it could be avoided by any other means. If they were nevertheless determined to proceed in law, Robinson's expression was (according to the contemporary Alford diarist Robert Mason) that "they should have a beliful."

Titus Bourne had taken over from William Carnley not only the successful legal practice but also the various influential appointments he had had in the town. So Titus Bourne became Steward of Alford and Orby and various other local manorial courts, Secretary to the Association for the Prosecution of Felons and Clerk to the Alford Court of Requests. He was also appointed Clerk to the Commissioners of Property Tax in 1807. For quite a number of years he was practising in partnership as Bourne & Carnley, with William Carnley Junior. But the younger Carnley is only a shadowy figure in the records and appears to have dropped out of the partnership about 1830. In 1841 he died.

For some years after 1805 the practice seems to have carried on from the High Street premises belonging to the Carnleys but Bourne eventually bought and renovated substantial premises in West Street. The building had an imposing frontage and was a very large one, as it needed to be since Bourne and his wife Margaret had 13 children. Several servants also lived on the premises; there were four indoor servants even

15. Titus Bourne's house in West Street, Alford which was converted to shop premises shortly after his death. The former legal office (to the right) was, as was usual at the time, only an appendage to the main building.

at the time of the 1851 Census when the children had all flown the nest. And in the typical manner of the time the relatively small office premises formed an extension adjoining the house itself. Titus Bourne was also a banker and indeed it was the banking part of his practice that he most enjoyed and concentrated on. The legal branch of the business he largely left to his younger partners. And he always seems also to have had loyal, long-serving staff. In particular William Sylvester ran the firm's insurance agency and seems to have been part-time Town Postmaster, while Thomas G. Marshall, after joining Bourne as a boy, understudied William Sylvester as managing clerk and, as Titus Bourne grew older, became responsible for the day-to-day running of the banking business.

The Bournes were related to the Tennysons through John Bourne of Dalby, Titus Bourne's cousin, having married Mary Tennyson, whose brother George, the Rector of Somersby, was the poet Alfred Tennyson's father. Alfred Tennyson's home life at Somersby was stressful and unhappy and, as Mary Bourne took the Tennyson children's part against their father,

16. Mary Bourne of Dalby

Dalby Hall was to them a second home. She was a forbidding figure of stern Calvinistic principles and Alfred Tennyson remembered

17. Alfred Tennyson as a young man

seeing her glaring at him across the street in Spilsby one day and shouting "this reminds me of the great gulf which shall divide the wicked from the blessed." She was, nevertheless, in these days also kindly and amusing and Titus Bourne's daughter Eliza remembered a late-night family gathering at Dalby Hall, when, the servants being in bed, Mary Bourne sent Alfred Tennyson down the cellar for wine, saying in joke "You must whistle all the time to show you are not drinking it." The garden at Dalby Hall was taken by the Bourne family to have been that to which Maud was invited in Tennyson's poem.

Mrs Tennyson of Somersby and her children were also very friendly with Titus Bourne's family at Alford. The two families spent a lot of time together at the seaside at Mablethorpe. Bourne's daughter Eliza remembered there being a great deal of smuggling on the Lincolnshire coast at that time and the young people sallying out in the evening to watch the smugglers on that lonely shore exchanging lights and landing their goods. She also recalled Alfred Tennyson's marked Lincolnshire

18. Mr and Mrs Titus Bourne's friend, Elizabeth Tennyson, the poet's mother

accent. He was particularly fond of her sisters Margaret and Alice, who were portrayed in his poems Margaret and Adeline, the latter name being a poetic rendering of Alice. Tennyson left Lincolnshire for the south in 1837 with his widowed mother and her younger children. However, some local recollections of the young Tennyson are of him as rather an eccentric figure and Margaret Bourne has been remembered as saying to a friend and near neighbour of her mother's "Oh Mrs Higgins can I come over to you this afternoon - that dreadful Mr. Tennyson is coming to Alford."

Titus Bourne's eldest son, Henry Titus, who had started work in the office at 16, became articled to his father and in 1835 joined him in

19. Titus Bourne's daughter Margaret, the subject of one of Tennyson's poems

the partnership Bourne & Son, largely taking over the legal practice and building up for himself a very good reputation in the town. Everything for the future was set fair. Henry Bourne took over or joined with his father in a number of clerkships and stewardships. And Bourne & Son were well placed to undertake a new kind of business that had arisen as a result of the spirit of reform having extended to politics. The 1832 Reform Act had extended profitable opportunities for well-established country solicitors as political agents.

In religion too reform movements were afoot. Religion and the Law had always gone forward together. As a seventeenth-century Judge had said "Christianity is parcel of the Laws of England." This was especially so in the Bournes' time. Wills had traditionally begun with the hallowed old invocation "In the Name of God Amen" and until 1858 Probate of Wills was still obtained under the Bishop's seal from the ecclesiastical Court at Lincoln.

The Georgian Church of England, however, though admirable in many ways, was indolent and it was Methodism that was the revitalising force of

English Christianity at that time. Titus Bourne was perhaps unusual among the prosperous country solicitors of those days in being a staunch Wesleyan Methodist. But the Bourne family had been Dissenters from generations back. Lincolnshire proved to be fertile ground for the growth of the new individualistic evangelical Protestantism. And in the Alford area Titus Bourne had a central role in Methodism's success. John Wesley himself had preached in Alford Market Place in 1788 but when Bourne came to live in Alford in 1805 there were only a handful of local Methodists holding their meetings in a private house in South Street. Bourne was a keen supporter of the British and Foreign Bible Society and his Bible Class was very influential. To the

20. John Wesley. The Bourne and Brackenbury families were strong local supporters

diarist Robert Mason it was a lifeline from the effects of his apprenticeship to a wicked shopmaster and the persecutions of a drunken father. In 1817 Bourne led the way in the building of the Methodist Chapel in Chapel Street. And by the time of his death the membership of Alford Methodist Circuit was 1,800 strong.

In 1843 the Stamford Mercury reported that the whole of Bourne's family, including married and single, were baptised by a clergyman of the Church of England and two of his sons eventually went on to become parsons. Titus Bourne himself remained a consistent Wesleyan, promoting his church and trying to improve conditions in the town. But, as his later partner Frederick Rhodes said, there was never anything like intolerance or sectarianism in his character and the good he did was not limited by any considerations of the denomination, either in religion or politics, to which the recipients of his bounty or his aid belonged.

For 20 years Titus Bourne and Henry Titus continued to practise together and then there was catastrophe. Henry Bourne suffered a complete and permanent mental breakdown. At 70 years old Titus Bourne had the stressful task of taking his firm forward. A new junior partner had urgently to be found. Although he had another son Septimus who was a qualified solicitor, Septimus was an invalid not really able to hold down a job. And while two of Bourne's daughters had married solicitor-brothers, these sons-in-law had their own established practice in Derbyshire. He therefore invited Frederick Rhodes, a youngish solicitor from Market Rasen, to join him at Alford, being aware that Rhodes's father's legal practice at Market Rasen was not on a scale to provide him with a future there.

According to Frederick Rhodes' reminiscences of him, Titus Bourne was a kindly old gentleman who had lived for many years in the esteem and affection of those by whom he was known, an interesting and genial companion and a warm-hearted friend. However, his life had been full of family sorrows experienced through early deaths and misfortunes of his children culminating in the tragedy of Henry's illness. People in the town thought, according to Robert Mason, that Bourne, being a sensitive and even nervous man, would have sunk under such heavy trials. But Bourne seems to have been an example of what G.M. Trevelyan called the seriousness of thought and self-discipline of character of the enthusiastic evangelical Protestants of his time and he went on in old age to have an Indian Summer.

Bourne's friendly well-organised approach to life can be seen in his letters to his diffident new young colleague. Having sounded out a doctor's widow, Mrs Tong, to see if she might take in Frederick Rhodes as a lodger, he wrote in October 1854 to Rhodes, who was preparing to come back to work after an early bout of illness "I fear the Lady to whom I referred tho' a Widow who has arrived to the venerable age of 66 or thereabouts feels too much Female Delicacy to take a Bachelor as a Boarder. She was in the House Henry inhabited ....the Vicar I find would gladly have you but I fear his Terms would be high........we have had a busy Business Market today at Spilsby. Orby Copyhold Court is fixed for Saturday the 20th. Could you meet me at Louth Sessions on the morning of the 24th to assist in the prosecuting I mentioned?"

Typically detailed instructions and encouragement later that year came in from Bourne who was touring over Christmas in Leicestershire and Lancashire on family visits "we fully propose getting home (DV) on Friday evening....- I am rather calculating upon leaving the Wainfleet sale to you and Marshall as it would be desirable for me to remain at home on the Saturday to balance my cash Accounts etc. Still, if it should be considered more desirable that I should attend to the sale, with reference first to the client's satisfaction also secondly as to the influence I might possibly have with any of the Purchasers regarding the preparation of Conveyances, I will endeavour to do so and in that case Mr Marshall must remain at home to attend to Banking Business which at the close of the week and the year must not be neglected. You should hear again from me after my arrival at Liverpool on this matter if I should feel it needful to say any more about it........I feel full confidence in committing to you (with Marshall's aid as to his knowledge of all our Land and Banking matters) the management of whatever may arise at Home assured that all will be properly disposed of........P.S. In the Presentment respecting the light butter the Name should be spel'd Burkitt not Birkett".

Bourne very much welcomed the new railways which enabled him to travel all over the country visiting his relatives, especially those in Derbyshire and in Lancashire where the Bourne family had originally sprung from. In his 70s his enthusiasm for his work, his home and his family was as keen as ever. Thus on an extensive summer tour in 1857 to Lancashire and Derbyshire from letters to Rhodes who had instructions to write to him at least once on each stop on his tour "I observe you keep moving on regularly with Business falling in and also with Arrears. You do not say whether you have heard from Dr Thompson which I am anxious to know…Mrs. Bourne and I spent a very pleasant and interesting Sunday here yesterday…- our youngest niece, a very clever girl and Teacher in a large Boarding School here took tea with and accompanied us to the Chapel. We heard a most excellent Discourse from a Preacher from Conference who was at Alford (his first circuit) many years ago.....the rain here yesterday and today is constant and heavy. I fear my Haystack will suffer for Want of the Thatch. I left full Orders with old Goodwin to secure it in Time if practicable but I cannot but have my Misgivings."

A very sociable man himself, Bourne was very active in promoting Rhodes's interest among his local friends and relatives and in the town. He was clearly keen that his practice should continue to flourish after he himself had gone and had made special provision in his Will to enable his beloved banking practice to remain part of the business.

Certainly Bourne and Rhodes did very well during the years when they were together in partnership, as surviving Income Tax papers show. Income Tax had first been introduced as a temporary measure to finance the Napoleonic Wars, being abolished after the victory at Waterloo. It was re-introduced in 1842, supposedly again on only a temporary basis, and went on gradually to replace the old Assessed Taxes. Income tax rates rocketed as a result of the 1854-56 Crimean War to a record nineteenth century 7%. Since the tax threshold was £100, there were only at this

ASSESSED TAXES.

ARMORIAL BEARINGS. Any person using or wearing any armorial bearing, where such person shall be chargeable with the duty for any carriage at the rate of 3*l.* 10*s.*, to pay annually 2*l.* 12*s.* 9*d.*—where such person shall not be so chargeable, 13*s.* 2*d.*

CARRIAGES. For every carriage with four wheels, drawn by two or more horses or mules, 3*l.* 10*s.* ; if drawn by one horse or mule, 2*l.* For every carriage with four wheels, each being of less diameter than thirty inches, and drawn by two or more ponies or mules, neither exceeding thirteen hands in height, 1*l.* 15*s.*; where the same shall be drawn by one such pony or mule only, 1*l.* For every carriage with less than four wheels, if drawn by two or more horses or mules, 2*l.* ; if drawn by one horse or mule, 15*s.* ; and where the same shall be drawn by one pony or mule only, not exceeding thirteen hands in height, 10*s.* ; and where such carriage shall be kept and used only for the purpose of being let for hire, one-half of the above-mentioned duties respectively. For every carriage used by any common carrier, and used only occasionally for conveying passengers for hire, where such carriage shall have four wheels, 2*l.* 6*s.* 8*d.* ; and where the same shall have less than four wheels, 1*l.* 6*s.* 8*d.*

Exemptions. Carriages used solely in the affairs of trade or husbandry, and whereon the name and address of the owner shall be legibly painted ; provided such carriage shall not be used for any purpose of pleasure, except for conveying the owners thereof or his family to or from any place of divine worship.

DOGS. For every dog, of whatever description or denomination the same may be, 12*s.* No person to be chargeable to any greater amount than 39*l.* 12*s.* for any number of hounds, or 9*l.* for any number of greyhounds, kept by him in one year.

Exemptions. Any dog which, at the time of returning the list of dogs, shall be under the age of six calendar months; dogs kept solely for the care of sheep or cattle ; provided no such dog shall be a greyhound, hound, pointer, setting-dog, spaniel, lurcher, or terrier.

GAME. Every deputed gamekeeper must take a certificate from the clerk of the peace, and pay annually 1*l.* 5*s.*—Every other person 3*l.* 13*s.*—Fee for the certificate, 1*s.*—— Any person killing game without a certificate, forfeits 20*l.*—Persons refusing to show their certificates, or to tell their names and places of abode to a person having a certificate, forfeit 50*l.*

Certificates do not exempt unqualified persons from the former laws.

Gamekeeper hunting out of his manor, is deemed to have no certificate.

DEALERS. Persons licensed to deal in Game are to take out a certificate, charged with a duty of 2*l.*; but certificated persons may sell Game to licensed dealers, if paying the duty of 3*l.* 13*s.* 6*d.*

HAIR-POWDER. Every person who shall have worn hair powder within the year preceding the term for which the assessment ought to be made, 1*l.* 3*s.* 6*d.*

Exemption. Any of the menial servants of her Majesty, or of any of the royal family.

HORSES. For every race horse, 3*l.* 17*s.* For every horse, and for every mule, exceeding respectively the height of thirteen hands, kept for the purpose of riding, or drawing any carriage chargeable with duty, 1*l.* 1*s.* For every such horse or mule, not chargeable as above, 10*s.* 6*d.* For every pony or mule, not exceeding the height of thirteen hands, kept for the purpose of riding, or drawing any carriage chargeable with duty, 10*s.* 6*d.* ; and for every such pony or mule kept for any other purpose, 5*s.* 3*d.*

Exemptions. Horses used for the purposes of husbandry, or for drawing any carriage not chargeable with duty, or for carrying burdens in the course of trade. Horses used in the trade or business of a market gardener. Ponies or mules not exceeding thirteen hands in height, and used solely in any underground mine. Horses used in her Majesty's service by officers or private soldiers.

SERVANT-MEN. Masters to pay annually for every male servant of the age of eighteen years or upwards, 1*l.* 1*s.* ; and for every such servant under the age of eighteen, 10*s.* 6*d.* For every under gardener, or under gamekeeper, 10*s.* 6*d.*

Exemptions. Officers in the army or navy, for as many male servants as are allowed to them by the regulations of the public service. Servant under the age of twenty-one years, being the son or grandson of, and residing with his employer.

21. Assessed Taxes of the kind payable by Titus Bourne and Frederick Rhodes

time 500,000 taxpayers across the country and, for small country town solicitors, the annual profits figures, for the years 1855, 1856 and 1857 of £545, £559 and £570 respectively showed a very satisfactory steady level of business. Most of the profit, which by 1859 was shared equally between the two partners, seems however to have come from the banking part of the practice. Bourne would, of course, have been additionally liable to Land Tax and for Assessed Taxes under several of the prescribed heads of duty.

Anonymously writing in 1859 the obituary notice of Bourne's death in the Stamford Mercury, Frederick Rhodes said that "when, some six months ago, he remarked at one of those assemblings of his friends which were held at regular intervals under his hospitable roof, that they would not look forward to many more, not one of those who heard him could listen to his words unmoved. Of the closing hours of his life but little must be said; rather let all respect be paid to the sacred privacy of such a scene. But we may say that he viewed his approaching dissolution with calmness and composure, and that, to use his own words, he committed his soul entirely 'to the captain of his salvation'". And Robert Mason thought the text of Alford's Methodist Minister's valedictory sermon very apposite "so teach us to number our days that we may apply our hearts unto wisdom." Bourne's body was buried at the entrance of the little churchyard at Dalby Park.

22. Alford in the early 19th Century viewed from across the fields

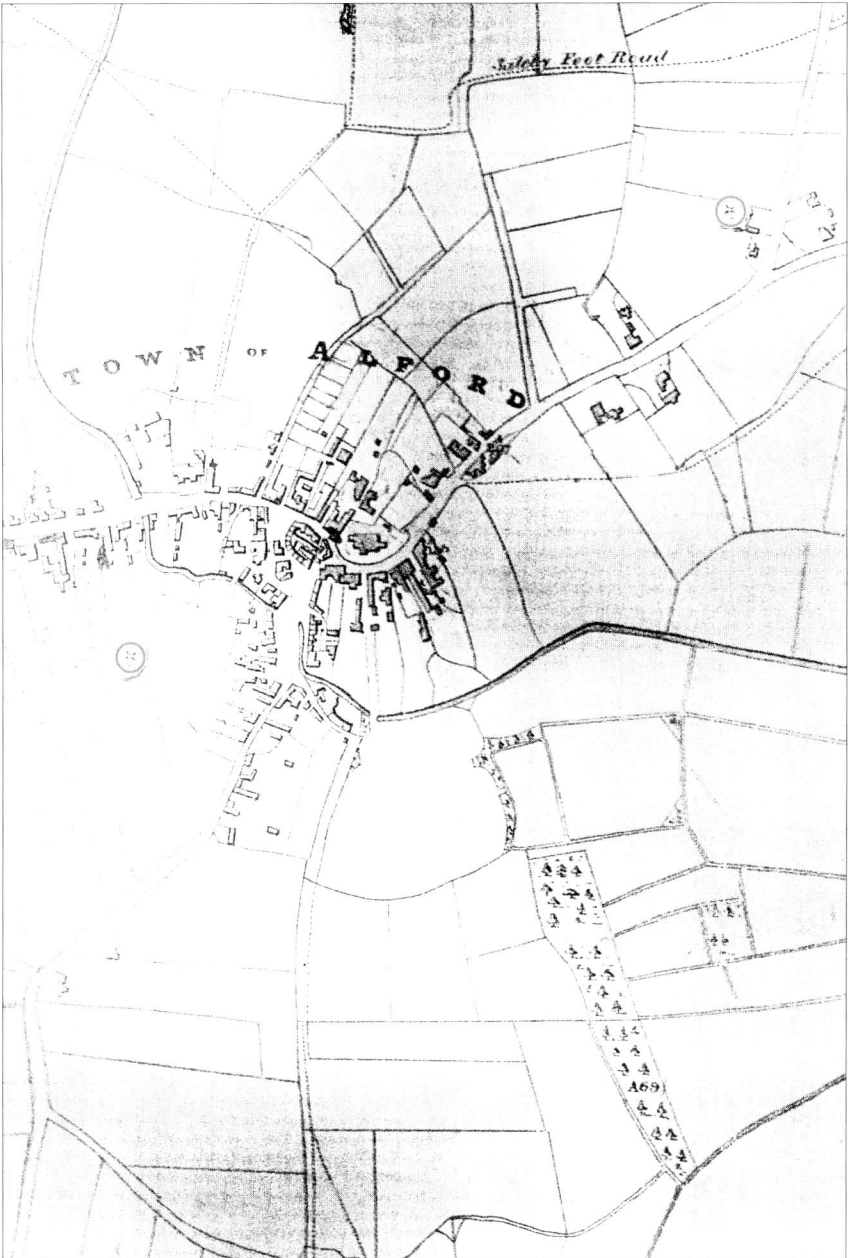

23. Alford Town Centre in 1841 after Enclosure but before the coming of the railway

CHAPTER THREE

Frederick Rhodes 1853-1894
in the Agricultural Depression

Frederick Jackson Rhodes was born in 1818. His father, Thomas Rhodes, was a solicitor in Market Rasen, who became well known as the district political agent and campaign organiser for Sir Montague Cholmeley, the Liberal M.P. for the north of the county. The family was a large one and, while two or three of the boys wanted to follow their father into the Law, his practice at Market Rasen was not large enough to have an opening for more than one son to have a future with him there.

Even in the early nineteenth century, prospective solicitors still did not have to face written examination of their legal knowledge before being able to practise. But, just as Frederick Rhodes was leaving school at Louth, the Law Society had at last arranged for formal testing of candidates for admission as solicitors to start from 1836. The early examinations, and indeed those right on into the early twentieth century, seem, from today's viewpoint, to have been marvellously old-fashioned. Candidates were given credit for listing the books they had read on the subject being examined and "question-spotting" was easy. An examinee in 1905 told the writer that he had confidently prepared very thoroughly for a question to come up on rights as to occupation of church pews. It did and, he said, he was home and dry.

It was to be quite some time before Frederick Rhodes actually qualified as a solicitor. He was articled to his father for the usual 5 years, one of which was spent with a conveyancing barrister at Gray's Inn, but, apart from this brief spell in London, he seems to have been living at home and working for his father for 15 years or more, for most of them effectively managing the Market Rasen practice.

THE LAW SOCIETY OF THE UNITED KINGDOM

27*th October*, 1848.

SIR,

I AM directed, by the Examiners appointed for the Examination of Persons applying to be admitted Attorneys, to inform you that you are required to attend on *Tuesday*, the 14th day of *November* next, at Half-past Nine in the Forenoon, at the Hall of the Incorporated Law Society, in Chancery Lane, in order to be examined. The Examination will commence at Ten o'clock precisely.

I have to remind you that your Articles of Clerkship and Assignment, if any, with Answers to the Questions as to due Service, according to the Regulations approved by the Judges, must be left with me on or *before Thursday*, the 9th day of *November*, at 4 o'clock.

I am, SIR, your very obedient servant,

R. MAUGHAM,
Secretary.

₊ Where the Articles have not expired, but will expire during the Term, the Candidate may be examined conditionally, but the Articles must be left within the first seven days of Term, and Answers up to that time.

☞ The Examiners have desired me to add the following regulation : —

A paper of Questions will be delivered to each Candidate, containing questions to be answered in writing, classed under the several heads of — 1. Preliminary. 2. Common and Statute Law, and Practice of the Courts. 3. Conveyancing. 4. Equity, and Practice of the Courts. 5. Bankruptcy, and Practice of the Courts. 6. Criminal Law, and Proceedings before Justices of the Peace.

Each Candidate is required to answer *all* the Preliminary Questions (No. 1.) ; and it is expected that he should answer in *three* or more of the other heads of inquiry. — *Common Law* and *Equity* being two thereof.

24. Frederick Rhodes sat for the Law Society's Examinations just a few years after their introduction and the exam syllabus is set out in this letter requiring his attendance

At 32 years old Rhodes was finally admitted as a solicitor and it was then time for him to look for a job away from home, so that his position at Market Rasen could be relinquished to one of his brothers. Suitable jobs in the Law for men of his age were not easy to come by. In the letters representing his CV he had been saying that he "conceived steady attention and business habits are qualities which would be considered the highest recommendation" but one firm bluntly rebuffed him saying firms were not so much seeking "an experienced and efficient man as a promising youngster whom they may mould in their own fashion". Eventually Rhodes obtained a temporary position as Managing Clerk to a Horncastle solicitor for a year at a salary of £175 but he became ill very shortly after starting work and the job only lasted a few weeks. So it was a wonderful opportunity for Frederick Rhodes when Titus Bourne, as a result of his son's collapsed health, suddenly needed a potential partner urgently for his Alford practice.

The splendid prospects at Alford were nevertheless daunting for a man of Frederick Rhodes' background and temperament. He was a Backroom Boy and Titus Bourne was so very much at the centre of business and social life in Alford and its part of the county. Soon after coming to Alford, Rhodes became ill and had to return to Market Rasen. But Bourne seems to have understood and valued his nervous new colleague, upon whom he was in any case dependent for the taking forward of his practice. In introducing Rhodes to the work and the town, he was always, as Rhodes recognised, "a kind friend" and he would surely have been upset to know that, on one or two occasions in his early days at Alford, Rhodes was continuing to look for jobs elsewhere. This however, appears to have been at the instigation of Rhodes' then intended fiancee. In a letter in the summer of 1853 she had expressed her feelings: "I was not a little surprised to find the partnership (of which you had before told me was in Lincolnshire) was at Alford. I thought perhaps it was at Holbeach or at Grimsby. I never once thought it was 'a place like Alford'. It seems very funny to think of living there of all places in the world. It's a wretched little place, one that nothing less than being 'your dear little wife' would induce me to live there". For whatever reason, whether through Bourne's solicitude he came to appreciate Alford

25. The house near Alford's East Street windmill where Frederick Rhodes lived for 40 years, first as Mrs Tong's lodger and then as tenant of her heirs

and his prospects there or he had never really agreed with his intended's strictures or he simply could find no satisfactory alternative future elsewhere, Frederick Rhodes finally decided to make his future in Alford. And, although the Intended was reconciled to the idea of living in the town, he no longer wished for the proposed marriage. Instead he settled in at the lodgings Titus Bourne had found for him with the doctor's widow, Mrs. Tong, and he continued to live there, as tenant of Mrs. Tong's beneficiaries after her death, until his own death 40 years later.

Alford was certainly at this time beginning to take shape as a pleasant, unpretentiously prosperous little market town. Its population had more than doubled since 1801 and it was typical of other small English country towns in providing virtually all the trades and services required for its own population and people in the villages round about. There were windmills, breweries and ropewalks. Gas had come to Alford in 1836 and even smaller local places such as Burgh-le-Marsh and Hogsthorpe eventually had their own gasworks. The arrival of the railway in 1848 had linked the town up with other parts of the country. And, just as elsewhere in England, substantial new public buildings were indications of progress. A Police Station and Court House was built in 1844 and over the next 20 years or so a Mechanics Institute, a Corn Exchange, a big new brewery, two National Schools, one for girls and one for boys, and three large new chapels for the various branches of Methodism.

So Frederick Rhodes had inherited from Bourne the successful solicitors' and banking practices and also the very central position in the management of Alford's institutions and public affairs. The challenge was, however, an awesome one. Rhodes' father, Thomas, helped with letters of encouragement and advice about "the great loss you will sustain in being deprived of so amiable and excellent a partner and friend..... Although he has taken very little off your shoulders lately, I think you must prepare yourself for some decrease in the Banking business, for to some of your Bank customers you can hardly be Bourne and it requires many years to establish a character and to gain sufficient confidence in a neighbourhood to be entrusted with monies to the extent to which your much esteemed partner has been. In your Profession too you may perhaps lose some few clients but this will be met by as many or more new ones for death always makes change of this sort.....You do quite right in keeping the name of your deceased partner in connexion with your own as regards the law business. If I were in your place I should hardly know when to give it up".

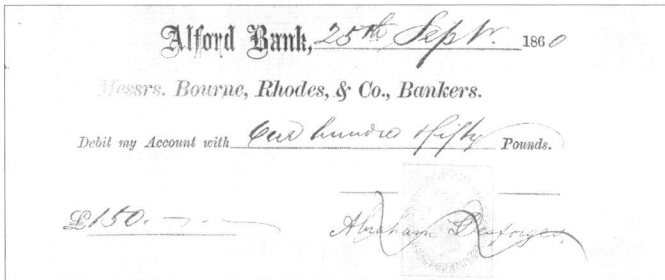

26. The banking practice unfortunately did not long survive Titus Bourne's death

Bourne had left everything well set up, particularly with regard to the Bank. Garfits, the large private bank at Boston, were very supportive, as were many influential clients. Even so Rhodes made a very bad start. He fell out with Thomas Marshall, the firm's long-serving Managing Clerk, who was the anchorman of the practice and had for some time effectively been running the Bank. Marshall had expected to be made a partner in the banking practice with Rhodes and Mrs. Titus Bourne and left when the partnership was not forthcoming. With his departure it was not possible to continue with the Bank which had to be sold. Mrs. Bourne then decided to sell the West Street premises. So Rhodes was left without an office and with income only from the legal practice which had not been as profitable as the banking one. For a short period he joined forces with another Alford solicitor, L.J. Brackenbury, but Brackenbury was not a good businessman and the association was not a success.

Despite his prominent position in the town, Rhodes's life, as the little diaries he kept up in virtually illegible handwriting each year show, was a hard and lonely one. He was conscientious and industrious to a fault. According to his diaries, he commonly "sat close all day", writing letters, perusing papers and seeing the occasional client. Reading, and walking by himself on summer evenings, were his recreations and any time he had away from Alford was spent at Market Rasen attending to work at his father's office. On a couple of occasions he was much smitten by the charms of young ladies and wistfully recorded in his diaries their having found husbands of their own age. So, with pressure of work and personal isolation, his perspective was naturally a narrow one. The diaries punctiliously account for purchases of lunchtime penny buns and such things as threepenny haircuts. But he was not well-organised as to the financial or general direction of his business. And, in some of the important appointments he held in local administration, for example as Manorial Court Steward or as Clerk to the Local Board of Health (the embryo local authority), he was not always sensitive to unpopular consequences of his decisions.

27. Country solicitors of Frederick Rhodes's time were involved in local organisations of all kinds for example Rhodes's membership of the Alford Agricultural Labourers' Society

Rhodes however was clearly a thoroughly decent and dutiful man. Clients spoke of him as a man of strict integrity and as a thoughtful and methodical man of business. He was a regular attender at the Parish Church where he was a sidesman, helped with the Sunday School and was on the local Bible Society Committee. When the church was renovated by Sir George Gilbert Scott in 1868 (services being held at the Corn Exchange at this time), he organised the Church Restoration Committee's meetings at his office. And, with the Vicar, he was involved in the Vestry Meeting, which, before the 1894 local government reforms, was the authority not only for church's affairs but for the town's. He was also much engaged in educational matters, being the last Bursar and first Clerk to the Governors of the Grammar School and also legal adviser and man of business for Alford's National Schools, and he was a founder-member of the Lincolnshire Law Society on its formation in 1879. Like Titus Bourne, he was personally a Liberal but did not concern himself actively in party politics.

A particular source of strength for Rhodes was the good relationships he maintained with the families of his predecessors in his firm. His landlady, Mrs Eliza Tong, had been very friendly with both Mrs. Titus Bourne and the Carnleys. Many members of the influential Bourne family stayed with Rhodes as their solicitor throughout his long career, despite the fact that two of Bourne's daughters were married to solicitor-brothers with their own firm in Derbyshire. And Rhodes kept very much in touch with the Carnley family through William Carnley of East Torrington, the farmer son and grandson of the firm's earlier principals. In 1858 he was writing

28. William Carnley of Torrington, later of Bilsby, S.B. Carnley's father, 'a fine sportsman' according to his son's inscription on this oil painting

29. Shortly after this photograph was taken in 1865 the High Street premises were transferred to Frederick Rhodes by Sidney Carnley's father, having been for many years purely a private residence of the Carnley family

to thank Rhodes "for a barrel of oysters received yesterday which are very acceptable at this season" and William Carnley eventually seems to have had in mind from an early stage that one of his sons, Sidney, might take up the Law and renew the family's old connection with the Alford practice. So, in Sidney Carnley's boyhood, Frederick Rhodes and his father were able to plan out the future to their mutual advantage. In 1873, when Sidney Carnley was still only 13 years old, William Carnley sold Rhodes the High Street premises, where the practice's office had been 70 years before and which had since been the private residence of various Carnley relatives. In this way, Rhodes solved the problem he had had in having no suitable office premises. Three years later Sidney Carnley seems to have left school early and come to work at the office. At 18 years old Carnley became articled to Rhodes and shortly afterwards Rhodes was already talking with his father about future partnership terms. Then in 1883, almost immediately after Sidney Carnley had completed his articles and passed his Finals, the partnership commenced.

Rhodes had done well to secure the future of the practice in this way, although the partners of the Rhodes & Carnley practice were seemingly a most incongruous pair. Rhodes was modest and rather nervous and introspective whereas young Sidney Carnley's personality was exceedingly strong-headed and even belligerent. However, Rhodes, being so very much older, having the background connection with his father and

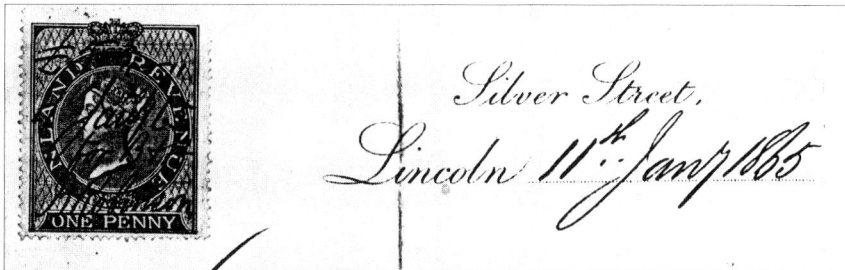

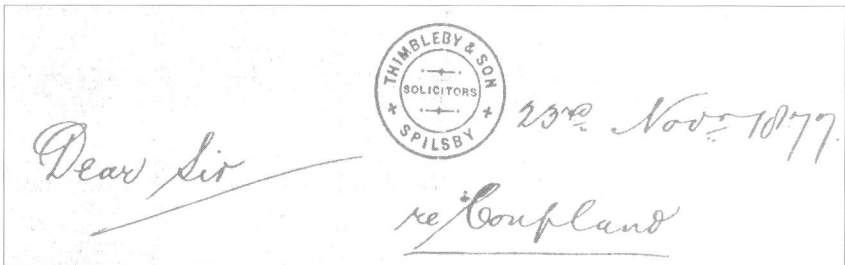

30. Early letterheads of country legal practices were either rubber stamped (above) or had a printed address only (top)

31. A 'Legal Nest' of japanned boxes, the eighteenth and nineteenth century precursor of modern filing cabinets

perhaps through his very diffidence, seems to have been able to cope with Carnley's training.

In any event, with Rhodes being 65 when Carnley got his partnership, it was natural that the younger man should quickly take over the direction of the firm. This was all the more important because the second half of the nineteenth century saw challenging processes of modernisation for solicitors' offices. Telegraph services had first become available in 1850 and by 1883 were in general use. The volume of postal correspondence had greatly increased with the coming of the Penny Post and the railways. Some firms were beginning to use simple stamped or printed letterheads and shorthand was by now commonly in use. Even filing systems were becoming more efficient. Copying presses were installed to duplicate the letters (Rhodes's diary mentions a new one being acquired in 1858) and 'legal nests' were introduced to stack up the black japanned boxes of documents of important clients whose names imposingly appeared on them. Such boxes, marked 'Sir Leicester Dedlock Baronet' and 'Manor of Chesney Wold', fascinated visitors to the Dickensian solicitor, Mr. Tulkinghorn, in Bleak House and a legal nest of this time remains in use at Alford. The modern type of filing cabinet began to appear in the 1890s and in 1885 Carnley spent the then large sum of £84 on the construction of a walk-in flint-shelved fireproof safe. By 1883 typewriters and telephones had also actually been invented, although it was to be another 30 years or so before the legal profession had them in general use.

Carnley's strong young hand taking over the direction of the firm was all the more necessary because, just at the time he came over to work with Rhodes, the English countryside was experiencing the effects of the terrible Agricultural Depression. This was the delayed result of Corn Law Repeal in 1846 which had abolished the protected prices British farmers received for their harvests. At the time Sir Robert Peel's government had removed Corn Law protection, Disraeli had warned that this would eventually result in the ruin of British agriculture and, as early as 1849, Robert Mason was recording in his diary that "the agricultural interest in this county has been in such a depressed state since the protection of the Government has been abolished, the produce is selling at such low rates the farmer cannot pay his demands and, if the farmer cannot live, the tradesmen must eventually fall". Temporary recoveries kept agriculture generally prosperous until the crisis year of 1873-74. Thereafter the Great Depression continued without let-up for 10 years. Unremitting bad weather resulted in bad harvests but corn prices had to remain low because of cheap imports coming in to feed British cities from North America and Russia.

On Carnley becoming a partner in 1883, he efficiently kept track of his firm's financial progress and his net profit figures for the years 1883-1906 illustrate how well he kept the practice going. In particular, they show how he surmounted the second wave of the depression in the last decade of the nineteenth century and even the effect of the worst of the depression in 1895 can be seen in his figures. His files cover scores of insolvency cases of this period. But with Frederick Rhodes's foresight and planning and Sidney Carnley's firm direction the practice had survived and prospered in a period of continued economic crisis when so many local businesses, solicitors' practices among them, went under.

Recovery During the Agricultural Depression - S.B. Carnley's Net Profit Figures 1883-1905

32. Very many country businesses, including legal practices, went under in the Great Agricultural Depression during the last quarter of the nineteenth century but these figures show how the young S.B. Carnley, after becoming a partner in the midst of the Depression, successfully built up his practice over the following years

33. Alford in 1887

However, while his firm had so well succeeded, Rhodes' death in 1894 at the height of the crisis revealed that he personally had been ruined by the Great Depression. Like many country solicitors of his generation, he was not aware of the importance of accounts and bookkeeping. Old-fashioned solicitors had not really needed to be. They were like the solicitor described by Richard Jefferies in Hodge and his Masters: "He helped Frank to get into a large farm, advancing the money with which to work it. He ran no risk; for, of course, he had Frank tight in the grip of his legal fist. The secret was this - the lawyer paid his clients 4% for the safe investment of their money. Frank worked the farm.... and realised some fifteen or perhaps twenty per cent of which the lawyer took the larger share". But one dreadful effect of the Agricultural Depression was what we would now call Negative Equity. Over the years 1880-1886 agricultural property values collapsed. And so, when farmers became bankrupt and their farms had to be sold, there was not enough to satisfy the security of lenders under their mortgages. In so many of such cases, the lenders were solicitor-trustees such as Rhodes and in his own case his position was exacerbated by his very haphazardly informal accounting methods.

It seems quite probable from the surviving papers that, when Frederick Rhodes died in November 1894, he was unaware that he was personally insolvent. And upon his death, Carnley had immediately to remove the name Rhodes from their firm's practising title.

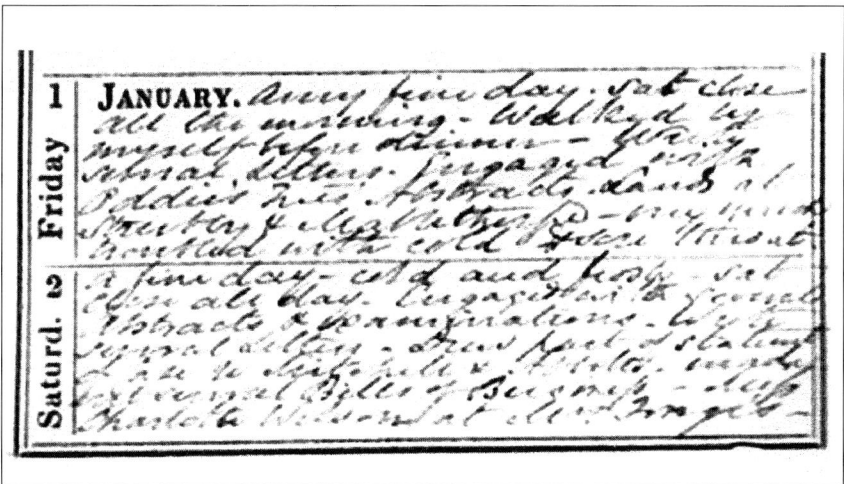

34. Entries from Frederick Rhodes's little diaries… in 1858

JANUARY.

This pocket Book — — 2 6
Hair cutting — — 6
Razors sharpening — 4
A quarter washing — 15 —

126 MAZAWATTEE COFFEE is simply   the highest class Coffee obtainable. 127

4 Sunday. NOVEMBER, 1894.
    24th Sunday after Trinity.
October accounts

8 THURSDAY.   NOVEMBER, 1894.

5 MONDAY.
    Moon, First Quarter, 3.16 p.m.

9 FRIDAY.

6 TUESDAY.

10 SATURDAY.

7 WEDNESDAY.

MAZAWATTEE TEAS, in 1, ½, & ¼ lb. pkts., and   in 3, 6, & 10 lb. tins, of leading Grocers everywhere.

35… and the final ones in 1894

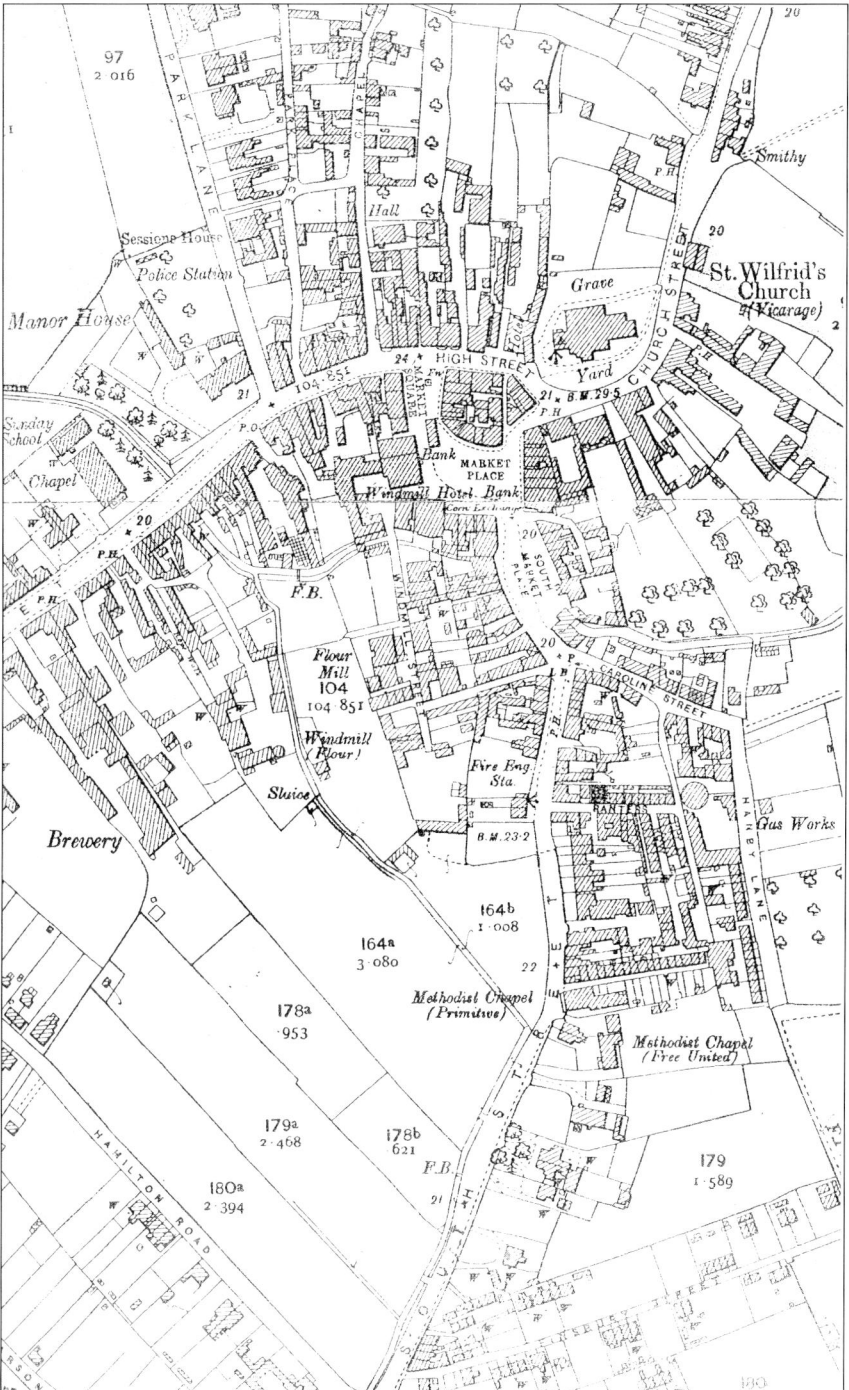

36. Alford in 1906

CHAPTER FOUR

S.B. Carnley 1876-1947 and the Impact of Two World Wars

Ever since he was a boy growing up on his father's farm at East Torrington Sidney Bazalgette Carnley had had an exceptionally powerful personality and this was in an age when there were very many more strong characters around than there are today. Coming over to Alford as a young teenager to work with Frederick Rhodes and spending the rest of his long life in the little town, he had plenty of scope to make his mark and he did so.

37. The young S.B. Carnley as a cricketer

As a young man, S.B. Carnley was prominent at Alford as a keen all-round sportsman. But modesty was never part of his make-up. Biographical notes he made for a newspaper article told of him as a cricketer carrying his bat through an entire innings thrice in one week and capturing five wickets in five successive balls in one over, at billiards winning a well-known tournament as a back marker 50 behind scratch, playing at full back in the F.A. Cup competition, as a figure skater able to write his own name on the ice, as a wing-game shot above average and as 'no mean performer with the gloves'.

Economic conditions in the countryside were very hard at the time Carnley entered into his partnership with Rhodes and the 1883 Partnership Agreement had to be on the basis that 'by reason of the long continued and present agricultural depression in the neighbourhood of Alford and Spilsby and the consequent paucity of business..... the future gains and profits of the said partnership cannot be estimated with any degree of exactitude'. The partners did, however, make a net profit of £238 each in their first year and Carnley, taking over more or less at once the management of the firm, proceeded from the first on a sound financial basis. Indeed he immediately made investments for the future. Having purchased the office premises from Rhodes, he spent £235 building two large new rooms at the back and he spent the then very large sum of £1,100 building a big house, next door to the new Grammar School, for him and his newly-wedded wife, the daughter of a local farmer, to live in.

38. Norbury House, the big new residence Carnley built for himself in 1883.

Carnley's working career at Alford from 1876 lasted for over 70 years and that whole period has been regarded as a time when business for solicitors across the whole country in general stagnated. But Alford itself, as the town's historian of Industrial Archaeology, G.B. Wood, has noted, probably reached its peak of prosperity in the years 1885-1910. S.B. Carnley was then himself in his energetic prime and his impact on local affairs was clearly to some degree responsible for the town's success. There had indeed been a feeling that the town, with its decreasing population, was in decline and, as the Lincolnshire Times flatteringly had it in 1904, S.B. Carnley was 'a vigorous compelling figure in this struggle for a new existence for the town whose example and infectious energy stamp him as just the personage needed to force upon the minds of his fellows that Alford is in a critical state and cannot be allowed to deteriorate further .... marked as a leader who attracts note by his loyalty to his town and his belief in the future of his community.'

His own playing days over, Carnley continued to be a keen supporter of the local cricket and football clubs but, outside of his work, he proceeded to indulge what he called the natural and inherent love of horses, brought about, he thought, from his surroundings in childhood, by establishing in 1891 a stud for the competitive breeding of Hackneys. This was extremely successful. One famous horse, Norbury Squire, won over 150 first and champion prizes including the 1896 World Trotting Championships and his Hackneys were sought for far afield, a particular market for them being with 'the plucky little Japs, the most enterprising nation in the world', as Carnley put it in 1905, reflecting the widespread admiration for the Japanese felt across Britain after their victory as underdogs in the Russo-Japanese War.

39. Carnley's famous prize-winning Hackney Norbury Squire

After establishing his stud, Carnley went on to found the highly successful Alford Horse and Foal Show, held in August each year, and a few years later he had a further great success in promoting the town with the establishment of an annual Lincoln Red Bull Fair. And these popular ventures were followed by Carnley taking the initiative in setting up the Alford Tradesmen's and Farmers Association to protect the interests not only of the town but also of isolated village shopkeepers and other small businessmen who might otherwise have felt entirely at the mercy of outside events. To them he was a formidable champion and he would at the drop of a hat lead a deputation to London to beard local MPs on the members' behalf.

NATIONAL HORSE BREEDING.

SEASON 1918.

AT the Hackney Society's Show, held at New-market on 8th March, 1918, the Judges of the class for Stallions most suitable for getting Army Horses were selected by the Director of Remounts for the War Office.

In a class of 16 Stallions

THE CUB,

12750 H.S.B., 5 years old,
WAS PLACED FIFTH.

DESCRIPTION.

The Cub is a golden chestnut, standing 15.3—the ideal Army height—with beautiful outlook and riding front and shoulders. He is on short, good legs, ample bone, knees and hocks near to the ground, and sound feet, with a back, loin and quarters to carry 17 stones. He is perfectly quiet under saddle, good tempered, and walks five miles an hour.

SOUNDNESS.

It is admitted by the equine world that the English Hackney is the soundest of all breeds. The Cub holds the Board of Agriculture certificate on this head.

BREEDING.

SIRE, Leopard 9783.
DAM, 19128 Grandford Sunshine.
Leopard 9783 by Leopold 8218 by Polonius 4931 by Wildfire 1224 (Wreghitt's).
19128 Grandford Sunshine by Copalder Gabriel 8105 by Stow Gabriel 5416 by Ganymede 2076.
To the student of pedigree it will be apparent that The Cub has none but the best of the old Hackney strains of blood, from Old Lord Derby 415, Confidence 158, and back to Triffitt's Fire-away in 1859, Achilles in 1854, and Performer in 1843.

FREE NOMINATIONS.

I am prepared to give 20 FREE NOMINA-TIONS for approved mares to Lincolnshire far-mers not exceeding 50 acres in occupation; these to be dealt with strictly in order of written application.

GENERAL FEE.

Approved Mares, £1, prepaid.

NOTE.

The Cub's sire Leopard is the greatest living Hackney Sire, six of his progeny having realised £6000 (Six thousand pounds).
The Cub will be exhibited :—
ALFORD....TUESDAY, 23rd APRIL,
and at Spilsby, Louth and Horncastle on later dates to be notified, and will stand for the sea-son at the Norbury House Stud, Alford.

Apply to

13th April, 1918.   S. B. CARNLEY.

BREED FOR THE ARMY—
THE NATION—
and YOURSELF.

40. Carnley advertising as a horse breeder during the First World War

41. Carnley outside his groom's house, behind which were his paddocks and stables

Carnley's next enthusiasm was for Alford to have a permanent cattle market to enable it to compete effectively with nearby market towns but he had to campaign for this for nearly 10 years until he brought his idea to fruition in 1912. By no means everyone liked the manner in which he pressed for 'vital and radical change' to secure 'a revival of interest in the welfare of our town', although for most of his opponents it was the messenger they disliked rather than the message. And Carnley himself was not radical but extremely reactionary in believing that it was individual local inhabitants operating within traditional local institutions who should have the management of the town's affairs. He thoroughly objected to the increasing amount of legislation authorising outside interference in local matters. And, from its inception under the powers granted by the Local Government Act of 1894, he was in a state of almost perpetual conflict with the Urban District Council, which Alford, though only having a population under 3000, had just to look after the administration of the little town.

In local politics, his allies in the Traders' Association supported him in his battles with the Council and, since some of the elected Councillors themselves belonged to the Association, there was always a considerable minority of Council members who could be relied on for support. Upon the creation of the new Council, he managed to ring-fence his position as administrator of the town's cemetery from unwelcome interference and in 1896 he beat down the new Council in a dispute as to who was responsible for the Alford Fair. Concurrently he was confident of maintaining the Vicar and Churchwardens' authority over Alford's three National Schools and he was not daunted by the Council enlisting the increasingly powerful Charity Commissioners in its support. "It is well known" , he told his barrister on the case, "that the Charity Commissioners are not above attempting to get hold, or control the administration, of charities which are distinctly outside their powers and when firm resistance is shown that body invariably suggests 'halves' with a view to getting in 'the thin end of the wedge.' " He boasted of a recent victory he had had over the Charity Commissioners' attempting to interfere in local affairs but in the matter of the Schools, although he took them right up to the High Court in London, the decision was eventually against him.

From feuding in local politics, Carnley went on to be involved in a series of tempestuous rows and scandals. His marriage was an unhappy one. His wife was an invalid and he was not at all a faithful husband. Among his many conquests was the daughter of another local solicitor. She lived next door to his house and for some years billets doux for assignations were placed in their boundary hedge. Indeed Carnley promised that, upon his wife's expected early death, he would marry the lady. But, by the time Mrs. Carnley died in 1906, he had become unwilling to proceed further in the matter. Meanwhile, the notes in the hedge had become violently hostile and even obscene and public attempts had been made to embarrass him in the town. Carnley was, however, virtually impossible to embarrass and matters came to a head when he was sued for damages for Breach of Promise of Marriage (an action open for women to take until 1970). Carnley argued that any promise he had made would not be enforceable as it would be against public policy on grounds of immorality for a married man to promise to marry another woman while his wife was still alive. And the Court of Appeal, overturning the original decision of the trial judge, eventually ruled that such a promise was indeed unenforceable and Wilson v Carnley became a leading case in its branch of the Law.

While the Wilson v Carnley case was at its height, Carnley was involved in an extremely bitter dispute on another front. He had been approached by a Boston solicitor to take into partnership his 25-year-old son, Geoffrey Staniland, whose elder brother already practised with his father at Boston.

Friday, Jan. 31.

(Before VAUGHAN WILLIAMS, FARWELL and KENNEDY, L.JJ.)

WILSON *v.* CARNLEY. (*a*)

APPEAL FROM THE KING'S BENCH DIVISION.

Contract—Promise of marriage—Promise to marry on death of defendant's wife — Knowledge of plaintiff that defendant was married—Illegality of contract—Public policy.

A promise made to a woman by a married man to marry her after the death of his wife, the woman being at the time of the promise aware that he was a married man, is against public policy, and is therefore void.

APPEAL by the defendant from the judgment of Lord Coleridge, K.C. sitting as commissioner of assize at Lincoln, on further consideration after the trial of the action with a jury.

The action was brought in respect of a breach of promise to marry.

The promise was made in 1894, the defendant being at the time, as the plaintiff knew, a married man.

42. Wilson v Carnley, a leading case of Breach of Promise of Marriage

Ambitious young solicitors of those days were looking for an income of £500 a year, eventually rising to £1,000, but partnerships were difficult to get even in a small country town. And they were expensive to pay for, the Alford office premises, contents and goodwill being valued at £6,000. Furthermore, in his negotiations with Staniland Senior, Carnley stressed that it 'should be clearly and thoroughly appreciated by the ingoer' that the position in his practice would be demanding. 'Very many younger men at the present day', he said, 'appear to think the world is made for them and not that they have to live in and on the world by their own individual exertions. The advancement of the office and practice must be made paramount to all other considerations, nothing must be considered too small and the sacrifices of personal convenience and considerations must always be borne in mind. Method and attention to detail are strongly urged. The present principal turns his hand to any portion of routine when required'. Geoffrey Staniland was undeterred and keen to get ahead. And when he came to Alford he clearly made an excellent impression in his job and in the town. But neither he nor his father seems to have at all appreciated what he was letting himself in for. Carnley was quite impossible to cope with either in the office or, with his boorish way of life, outside. So, after only 18 months, the partnership ended in disarray. Staniland went off to practise in a nearby town. And tragically, just a few years later, both he and his brother were killed in action in the 1914-18 War.

With the departure of Staniland, several influential public appointments were temporarily lost to Carnley's office. Another young solicitor, Thomas Loy, was now living in the town. He had filled the gap left by the illness and death of Lister Wilson of the old firm Wilson & Portington. With a steady reputation, so different from that of Carnley, he took over the Clerkships to the Urban District Council and to the Grammar School Governors from Staniland to add to his existing Clerkships to the Alford Magistrates and the local Commissioners of Taxes and practised in the town until his death in 1935.

43. Carnley in typically confident pose (with a friend) in the garden of Norbury House

Carnley's aggressive rudeness was indeed proverbial and it was exacerbated in periodic drinking bouts. On a notorious occasion he said to a pub landlord 'drinks all round, except for that man there', pointing rudely to a young serviceman in the corner. But he was paid back in kind when the serviceman, on his next leave, entered the pub saying 'drinks all round, except that man.', pointing to Carnley. Another prominent Alford resident told the writer he was 30 years late in keeping an appointment with the firm, it having been unilaterally fixed by a letter from Carnley reading simply 'Be at my office at 10 o'clock tomorrow morning' which had been deservedly ignored. And local pub landlords used to clear their bar counters of glasses and bottles later in the evening if Carnley were there as it was a habit of his suddenly to clear the counter of everything with his forearm. Very many people, in fact, found Carnley frightening and few dared try to restrain him. John Tinn (not at all frightened by Carnley) remembered going into the Magistrates' Court with him one day and a young policeman, new to the area, at the door, saying to Carnley 'take your hat off'. Carnley stopped, very slowly and deliberately looked the policeman up and down twice and then, ramming his Homburg further down on his head, stalked forward into the courtroom.

44. S.B. Carnley's office staff about the time he had taken over sole charge of his practice upon Frederick Rhodes's death

In 1913 indeed a newly arrived police Inspector did assemble evidence, charted on a plan, of Carnley's inebriated progress one evening through the town for charges in court about incidents occurring on the way. But, if Carnley was widely feared and disliked, he also had very many friends and admirers. And the Traders' and Farmers' Association in a press statement in response to the court case recorded its 'protest against and detestation of the methods recently employed by a small section of the community to strike a blow at the President of the Association and indirectly its members as a body 'and also place it on record' its vote of unabated confidence in the President of this Association who has done more than ever has been attempted by any other person for the welfare, prosperity and advancement of the town and trade of Alford and its neighbourhood'.

So reactions to the unbridled force of Carnley's personality were very mixed. On the one hand, he had the unpleasant characteristic of picking and then vindictively pursuing a long-term quarrel against inoffensive people who only wished to be on friendly terms with him, while on the other hand he would frequently champion with all his bull-headed forcefulness the causes of weak or unpopular people, especially if they found themselves up against the burgeoning powers of outside authorities. He very much followed the important principle for lawyers of acting without fear or

45. The office staff in 1897 (see also Appendix 2 on page 122)

favour in the proper case. And, when the National Agricultural Labourers' Union's Head Office wrote, diffidently wondering whether his connections with local farmers would prevent him taking on a member's case, Carnley replied that their local union representative 'knows my feelings of strict impartiality between master and man, as I act for quite as many men or even more than masters'.

In the Great War of 1914-18 Carnley became well known over a wide area for being prepared to act for people oppressed by the abuse of wartime emergency powers. Few solicitors wanted to act in such cases or to incur the unpopularity involved, which Carnley himself had no regard to. Typical of such cases were those of a conscripted soldier with 20 acres of land who had been given 26 days' leave in order to take up his potatoes and mangolds but needed an extension to enable him to plough and of an Alford shop-owner whose premises had been broken into by the requisitioning authorities. 'What was the urgency?' Carnley wrote to the War Office 'nothing - merely to get more office accommodation and as a fact they already had plenty but someone's whim suggested more'.

One of the most fraught of Carnley's 1914-18 War cases concerned a naturalised Englishman of German origin. He had settled in a nearby town to Alford nearly 10 years before the War, married a local girl and had a family of English children. And he had set up a business with scores of employees. But, with his German name, he and his family became during the War victims of the hysteria of those terrible times. First he was fined for one of his employees having left on a light in the blackout, incurring suspicions that this might have been done deliberately, then he received a Prohibition Order banning him from the East Coast area and requiring him to run his business from Yorkshire. Then he was compelled to leave his Yorkshire hotel, after the landlord had received objections to there being a German on the premises, and finally, as a British citizen, he received his call up papers. Carnley claimed exemption for him on the ground that his business was an important source of local employment and that he was needed to run it. The Chairman of the Tribunal, rejecting Carnley's argument, suggested that disregarding the business as a source of employment 'shows how patriotic the Local Tribunal has been in refusing exemption in spite of that and saying the man must go'. To which Carnley, as the press reported, witheringly replied 'It may be from your point of view but there is another epithet which might be applied to it with equal justice.' Carnley took matters up to the High Court but his long-standing London solicitor agent, who was necessary to bring the case, was not enthusiastic about having the business. 'If the matter is in anyway distasteful to you by all means say so', Carnley rebuked him 'but I am a great believer in getting wrong put right'. The London Agent then cooperated but was only able to get the required senior barrister to lead the sympathetic junior barrister, Mr Cohn, at high fees. 'I have done my best to get these fees reduced but I am entirely at his mercy', he wrote Carnley, 'I suppose the squeeze is put on because of the origin of the applicant'. In the event, the appeal failed and Carnley's client, by then in his 30s, was conscripted, though by that stage of the War a special labour battalion, not for service outside Britain, had been formed at the instigation of Mr Cohn for men, such as Carnley's client, of bicultural Anglo-German background, many of whom were, of course, Jews.

Court work with advocacy was the branch of law Carnley excelled at. Agricultural knowledge acquired in his youth had, he said, proved invaluable in the Courts, 'as many an opposing witness has found to his chagrin'. He particularly specialised in paternity cases, 'bairnswearing' as they were commonly called. Licensing was also important, as he acted for several local breweries. Country solicitors of his time invested a great deal of money on behalf of their clients and Carnley frequently chose breweries and pubs for investment. Some nimble footwork on his part was required when an elderly Methodist lady client of long standing wrote to say she noticed some money had been lent to brewers on mortgage in a pub and strongly objected in principle from deriving benefit from that source. The nature of Carnley's soothing reply can be gathered by her next letter saying that 'if the village inn is decent and well-conducted it is not objectionable for it is still a necessary institution and the rustic mind is far from being prepared for its abolition!'

After the terrible losses of the Great War everyone was anxious to get back to normal when peace came. But for country towns and country solicitors things would never really be the same again. Alford itself, as George Wood noted, went into something of a decline. There were indeed improvements, for example, in the telephone system and in the town's water supply, but small country towns like it saw their position as trading centres suffer from the increase of mobility motor transport introduced. And in the Law too there was radical change. Extensive new legislation in 1925 abolished the copyhold system of holding land, which Carnley right up to that time had been continuing to administer as Manorial Court Steward at Orby, and new simplified conveyancing procedures were introduced which solicitors of his generation found it hard to adjust to.

Nevertheless Carnley, in late middle age, was able to settle into a comfortable routine in his work at Alford and in the weekly attendances he

46. The building in front of Spilsby parish church in which Titus Bourne, Frederick Rhodes and S.B. Carnley successively had their office accommodation for 100 years prior to the demolition of the building in the 1920s

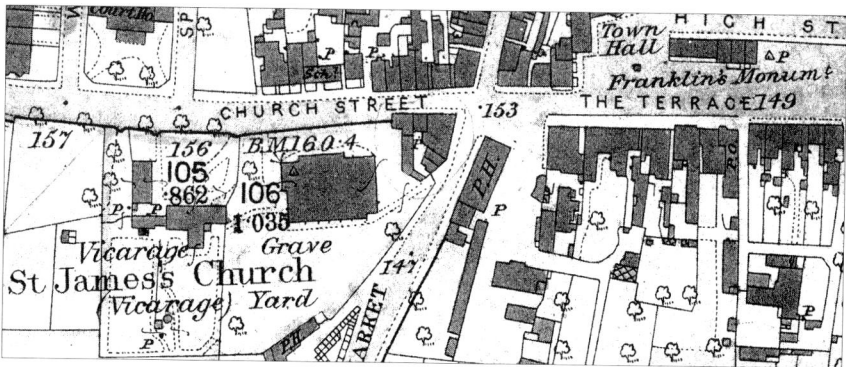

or his assistants made at his branch offices. His Spilsby office continued to be open on Mondays as it had been since Titus Bourne's time. There was also an office at Skegness, opened in the enthusiasm of Staniland's arrival at Alford, but this was discontinued in 1931. Thursday Market Day attendances were made at Burgh-le-Marsh and Mrs Hilda Middleton remembered regularly cycling the seven miles to and from Burgh to deputise for Carnley. Herds of cattle on the roads converged on the town for the market and Mrs Middleton's prudent practice was to remove herself and her bicycle into a roadside field to let a drove go by. With several of the staff away on active service, she had joined the office during the War as what she called the first female 'office boy', although it had been quite common since about 1900 for women to be employed in legal offices in the cities and larger towns. It was, however, to be 1922 before there was the first woman solicitor.

Carnley's life was, of course, mainly concentrated on the office. He was certainly a dynamic leader. Like many employers of his day, his presence was a fierce one. Short shrift was given to anyone who was incompetent or whose face did not fit. The mild mannered Rhodes noted in his 1887 diary 'L___ dismissed from the office very summarily by Carnley'. Tom Tiffin, his chief cashier in the period 1901-1918 and later himself a substantial figure in the National Farmers' Union, was a great admirer of his methods. The not very original office motto (but those were simple days) was 'If a job's worth doing, it's worth doing well' and Carnley's warning shot for incompetence was to say that without improvement, 'the next train to King's Cross will suit you down to the ground'. Tiffin's successor, Robert Hornby, coming to work as a youngster during the War, spent his early days in the office pining to be 17 and

47. Tom Tiffin who later went on to have a distinguished career with the NFU

be able to get out to France, little knowing the horrors that he would find there after his call-up. On his return from the Army, he found it had helped to stand up to Carnley. When threatened one day with dismissal, he had simply said he would 'collect his pens' and go, collecting one's pens or being asked to collect them being the equivalent of today receiving one's P45. And, upon this, Carnley had backed down.

In his earlier days Carnley was 'rushing about the office at breakneck speed' but latterly he based himself more in his own room. All the other 10 or so rooms in the building were connected to it (but not each other) by speaking tubes so that he could whistle through on them when he wanted attention. There were generally some seven clerks, who wrote or typed their own letters, and two office juniors or typists. John Parsons, who worked in the General Office (or reception area) where clients came in from 1930 to 1936 as a junior, remembers that Carnley's appearance there 'at any time tended to cause a mild panic among the permanent occupants; one felt rather less 'permanent' when SB was in a bad mood'.

Office hours all over the country were long in those days, generally 9.00am

the undersigned arrived at the left the Office

Thursday 8/6/33.

No.	Name	Arrived	Left
1	R. A. Myers.	8.46.	7.25
2	J. E. Parsons	8.53.	7-25
3	N. Mouncy.	8.55	7.20.
4	P. S. Fulham	8.57	7. 3.
5	S. Baggley	8.58	7. 4
6	R. Hornby	9	6.40

Friday 9/6/33.

No.	Name	Arrived	Left
1	J. E. Parsons	8.52.	7-15
2	N. J. Mouncy.	8.55	7. 25
3	P. S. Fulham	8.56.	6.40
4	R. A. Myers.	8.59	7.20
5	S. Baggley	8.59	7. 10.
6	R. Hornby	9	6.30

Saturday 10/6/33

No.	Name	Arrived	Left
1	J. E. Parsons	8.45.	2.55.
2	S. Fulham	8.56.	3 —
3	R. A. Myers.	8.56.	2.30
4	N. Mouncy	9	3.15.
5	R. Hornby	9	2.15
6	S. Baggley.	9	2.10 from Litton

Monday 12/4/33.

No.	Name	Arrived	Left
1	J. E. Parsons	8.50.	6-40 By permission
2	R. Hornby	8.53	6.40
3	S. Fulham	8.55.	7 —
4	N. Mouncy	8.56.	7.55
5	R. A. Myers.	9 —	7.56
6	S. Baggley	9 —	7 —

48. Before the Second World War office hours were generally long as the extract from a checking-in book shows

to 7.00 or 8.00pm with Saturday morning worked as a matter of course. Carnley's office opened at 9 o'clock and each member of staff signed a check-in book, an annual bonus of £5 being paid to everyone who had never even been a minute late any day of the year. An early arrival at the office had to take the morning post up to Carnley's house. There he marked each letter with initials in thick blue pencil to show who was to deal with it. He himself came down to the office shortly after 11 o'clock. Before the Second World War, he went home for lunch but, with staff shortages during the War, he got into the way of staying in the office till the evening, not having anything to eat until 8 or 9p.m. Although overtime was paid for work in the office after 7.15pm, John Tinn recollected that it was made very difficult for anyone (apart from him) to leave before Carnley did, the only acceptable excuse being when attendance was required on a cricket or football pitch. Saturday work, officially to 1 pm, tended to go on till mid-afternoon and, as Carnley reminded an assistant solicitor, 'we have to work on the seventh day when pressed'.

With Carnley growing older, Robert Hornby, who had increasingly taken over the practice's management, was anxious to secure the long term future by the addition of a new partner. Several prospective new partners had been driven away over the years by Carnley's overbearing manner. But eventually a very able young solicitor, John Tinn, was recruited from Hull. Partnership terms were drawn up in 1938 on the basis of the firm's net profits having averaged £1,100 over the previous three years. And Carnley's prevarications about actually signing the Partnership Agreement having been overcome by an ultimatum, the practice went ahead under its new name, S.B. Carnley & Tinn. Almost immediately, however, with the outbreak of the Second World War, the 80-year-old Carnley was complaining in a letter to Tom Tiffin 'I had six good clerks and a partner, who was nicely getting into his stride, and now I have only two of the originals, and two younger ones - in addition to that the Military Authorities also claimed the partner....this puts me in queer street and impossible to leave the office either early or late.'

At the end of the Second World War there were only 13,000 solicitors left in practice, the lowest number for over 60 years, and many of these were old-timers standing in for younger colleagues in the forces. For 20 or 30 years after the War, in fact, solicitors perusing title deeds for the prescribed 30-year evidence of property ownership, watched particularly for mistakes in the period 1925-45, just because of people like Carnley, who had either not been happy with the new 1925 conveyancing procedures or

Telephone with Private Exchange to all
Departments HOLBORN 2468 (4 Lines)

Telegraphic and Cable Addresses :
For Butterworth & Co. : "BUTTERWORT, ESTRAND, LONDON."
For the Canadian Compy. : "BUTTERWORT, WINNIPEG."
For the Australian Compy. : "BUTTERWORT, SYDNEY."
For the Indian Compy. : "BUTTERWORT, CALCUTTA."
For the New Zealand Compy. : "BUTTERWORT, WELLINGTON "

Cable Code :
Western Union (Univ. Edition).

BUTTERWORTH & CO.
S. S. BOND.

Canada : BUTTERWORTH & Co. (CANADA) Ltd., 351/353. Langside St., Winnipeg.
Australia : BUTTERWORTH & Co. (AUSTRALIA) Ltd., 170, King Street. Sydney
India : BUTTERWORTH & Co. (INDIA) Ltd., 6. Hastings St., Calcutta.
New Zealand : BUTTERWORTH & Co. (AUSTRALIA) Ltd., 49/51, Ballance Street
Wellington.

BELL YARD,
TEMPLE BAR,
LONDON, W.C.2

May 3rd, 1926.

The New Conveyancing Bureau.

Dear Sir,

THE NEW CONVEYANCING BUREAU has only been in existence for a fortnight and our anticipation that it would perform the very services which the profession now so vitally need is already realised.

Here is a verbatim extract from a Solicitor's letter which is an *absolutely spontaneous and uninvited expression of his opinion :*

> *"We read with very great interest your letter of yester-day's date. We should like to take the first opportunity of writing and congratulating you on your wonderful enterprise and the inestimable boon it will be to all of us to be able to get in the course of a day or two a considered reply to any knotty point that may have arisen in the New Conveyancing.*

> *"All country practitioners, particularly those who are engaged in Conveyancing and Trust offices, are having an extremely anxious time and your generous help and assistance will be a great relief."*

That the New Conveyancing has placed an almost intolerable burden upon the profession is fully borne out by the numerous letters we have received since the opening of the year, and we are only too glad to be able to announce this additional facility for helping practitioners to clear up knotty points and complicated problems.

Full particulars of registration of membership of the Bureau will be sent on receipt of the enclosed postcard.

We are,

Yours faithfully,

49. Many solicitors like S.B. Carnley had difficulty in coming to terms with the revolutionary property legislation of 1925

had continued well past retirement age during the war. Legal ways were changing fast. Carnley, for instance, was the last solicitor in the practice to read out Wills to assembled relatives after a death in the style seen in films. And, above all, important legislation came in to regulate legal firms' accounting practices. Accounts rules had been tightening up even before the War and in 1946 the requirement that solicitors must have their accounts certified by outside auditors was finally implemented. Carnley was typical of the strong resistance there had been to this among solicitors. He strongly objected to anyone locally being able to inspect his confidential dealings with his clients. So John Tinn was able to mollify the old man by appointing his own family's accountants in Goole to audit the books.

Carnley was 85 years old at the end of the War and John Tinn, returning from the forces, was ready to take things forward in his own way. Carnley, in some ways ahead of his time, had up to then insisted on every fee-earning member of staff, including Tinn, keeping up a daily time-costing book of just what work had been done in the day, and each evening these books had to be assessed by him (or Tinn) for the costs each client had incurred. John Tinn had protested that an hour or two of each person's time was lost in this time-wasting procedure and that the larger firm he had come from in Hull would not have entertained the idea of it. But Carnley had been adamant. Coming back from the War John Tinn insisted the procedure be abolished and it was to be another 40 years or so before time-costing on Carnley's principles was, for better or worse, universally adopted by solicitors.

Two years of twilight followed, Carnley coming into the office but as far as possible being kept out of the clients' way and being, somewhat at least, a mellower figure in the town, walking around in his distinctive Homburg hat with his clumber spaniels. Then in 1947 he died. Unlike his predecessors Titus Bourne

50. John Tinn, the young solicitor from Hull, who joined S.B. Carnley in 1938

and Frederick Rhodes, Carnley had had no place for Christianity in his view of things. And he had expressly stipulated in his Will that 'upon my death no bell shall be tolled, no parson shall anywhere be employed, no ceremony shall take place, no blinds shall be drawn, no mourning apparel shall be worn and no memorial of any kind shall anywhere be recorded.'

PART TWO

LOCAL INSTITUTIONS OF DECENTRALISED GOVERNMENT

CHAPTER FIVE
Agriculture

The Open Fields

Right into the eighteenth century the best cornfields in England, the Midlands and East Anglia, were still for the most part unenclosed. Towns and villages still had their huge manorial open fields. There were sometimes two and sometimes three of these common arable fields, one of which was left to lie fallow every year in rotation. Each field was divided into strips, perhaps of half an acre or an acre each, and the strips were separated by 'balks' of unploughed grassland. Every owner, including the Lord of the Manor, was allotted a number of strips scattered throughout the common fields.

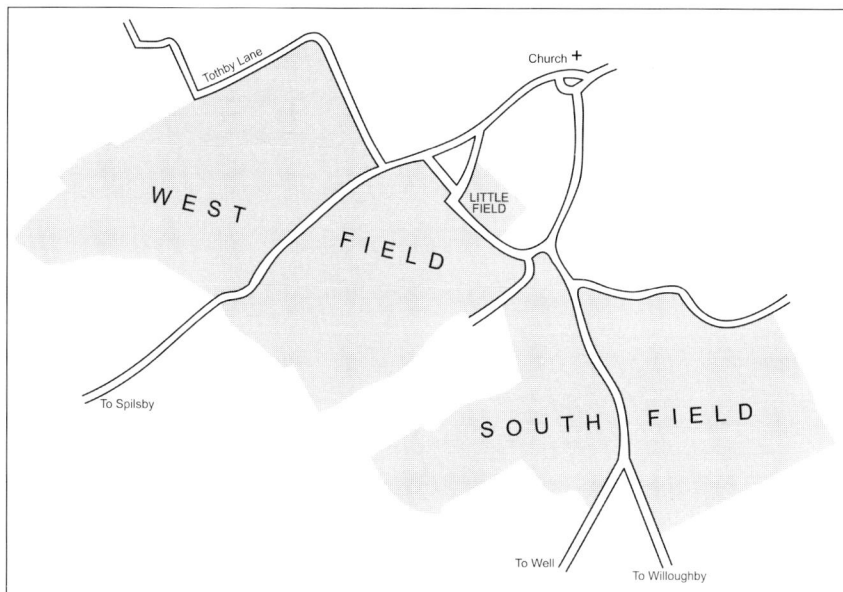

51. Alford's Common Fields: the Open Field system continued to operate at Alford well into the nineteenth century

Throughout the century and for many years afterwards Alford retained its open fields. The two big arable fields, the West Field and the South Field, with the Little Field, probably of cow pasture, in the centre of town, together contained a third of the agricultural area of the parish.

The method of cultivation of the common fields, what seeds were to be sown and when, and when the fields were to be opened for pasturage after harvest, was decided by agreement between the owners, traditionally at the Manorial Court. The Court also appointed the various officials to manage the common land, such as the Pinder, who shut up stray cattle in the Pinfold or Pound, and the Riders, who patrolled the fields to look after the ripened corn at harvest time.

With only a couple of breaks, the successive solicitors at Alford acted as Stewards of the Manorial Court there during four centuries. And a formal Agreement prepared by Titus Bourne in 1806 shows how the open fields were regulated at that comparatively late date. The West Field (except the land therein sown with beans and the pasture and meadow land therein) was to be sown with seed that present Spring and the South Field the same way in the Spring following and so on alternately during the continuance of the Agreement, thistles should be mown by each owner annually before 10th July upon pain of a fine for neglect and no beasts should be turned upon the land between 8th November and 1st May each year. Field Drivers were to be appointed to check the stocking of the field as they might think proper and there was to be a general Shepherd who should also be allowed to keep a horse upon the field free of charge.

Though rather anachronistic, the 1806 Agreement did indicate that the influence of the enclosure movement nationwide was already present even at Alford, for the number of owners of the common land had by then been reduced to only 8 and the Agreement stipulated that any sale or letting of land in the open fields should only be to one of the other parties to the Agreement.

Solicitors as Land Agents

Very large landed estates in the seventeenth and eighteenth centuries, as now, usually had full-time land agents employed to manage the estates. They were sometimes also at the same time stewards of the local manorial courts. And it was not unknown for a country lawyer to have started off in his career with a big landowner in this way.

Other landowners appointed one of their tenant-farmers to oversee their estates for them and some of these went on to become independent land agents dealing with a number of proprietors. Some indeed, with the opportunities that were opening up for land purchases, eventually became substantial landowners in their own right. In such a way the Bournes of Dalby had established themselves, first simply as graziers, then as land agents and ultimately as owners of the substantial Dalby property outside Alford. Until the end of the eighteenth century, most land agents were, however, solicitors. William Willerton and William Hardy acted for the local Christopher family's estate in this way and Hardy and Vaughan Bonner seem to have been solicitors and land agents to the Massingberd estate at South Ormsby and the estate of the Langtons of Langton.

Land agents were particularly useful when the estate proprietor lived outside the area. So when, at the death of Sir Robert Christopher, his estate passed to his daughter, Lady Sherard, and then on to his granddaughter the Duchess of Rutland and her Manners family heirs, Vaughan Bonner, Samuel Abbott, William Gonville and William Carnley successively looked after their East Lincolnshire estates.

The land agent, whatever his original qualifications, needed to have many skills, whether in agricultural or business management or in knowledge of the law. But, when

52. Lucy Duchess of Rutland, who inherited much of the land around Alford belonging to her grandfather, Sir Robert Christopher

the countryside came to be developed by road and canal building and land enclosures, surveying skills became increasingly important and gradually the predominant position of solicitors in land stewardship was lost. The career of the very influential Alford professional land agent, John Higgins, exemplifies this. On his arrival in Lincolnshire from Shropshire in 1819, he took over the management of the Manners estate and subsequently built up an extensive practice in Lincolnshire and beyond. And the independent position of his profession was eventually firmly established with the founding of the Institution of Surveyors in 1868.

LINCOLNSHIRE.

Particulars

AND CONDITIONS OF SALE

OF

THE WELL ESTATE,

Near ALFORD,

A VERY VALUABLE, COMPACT AND TRULY ELIGIBLE DOMAIN

OF

4,000 ACRES, and upwards,

FREEHOLD,

The greater part Tithe-free, and nearly in a Ring Fence;

COMPRISING

A MANSION HOUSE,

WITH SUITABLE OFFICES,

SURROUNDED BY ABOUT

300 ACRES OF GOOD PASTURE LAND;

Extensive Woods and Plantations; Eligible Farms, with Excellent Farm-Houses:

THE WHOLE CONTAINING UPWARDS OF

FOUR THOUSAND ACRES

Of Rich Arable, Meadow, Pasture and Wood

LAND,

Producing an INCOME (including the Profits of the Underwoods) of nearly

£.4,700 PER ANNUM;

A MODERN-BUILT AND WELL-SITUATED INN,

Several DWELLING-HOUSES and Shops in the Town of Alford;

THE TOLLS OF THE MARKETS AND FAIRS

Held in the Town of Alford;

EXTENSIVE MANORS,

Abundantly stored with Game; Courts Leet, Courts Baron, and other Royalties and Privileges; and

THE ADVOWSON

Of the United Rectory of Well-cum-Dexthorpe and Vicarage of Claxby:

Which will be Sold by Auction,

BY ORDER OF

The TRUSTEES of the late F. J. BATEMAN DASHWOOD, Esq.

BY MR. PEYTON,

AT GARRAWAY'S COFFEE-HOUSE,

CORNHILL, LONDON,

On WEDNESDAY, the 29th JUNE 1836, at 12 o'Clock.

53. When the Well Vale Estate was sold to RA Christopher it included a very substantial interest in the still-existing Common Fields

Enclosures

What at last facilitated the enclosure of Alford's Common Fields was the General Enclosure Act of 1836. This enabled a prescribed majority of the persons interested in common land to extinguish rights of commonage without specific Parliamentary approval. R.A. Christopher was in the course of purchasing the Well Vale estate, which included most of the common land, and since he and his six fellow proprietors were all in favour of enclosure, it was clearly common sense for them to be allotted coherent holdings.

John Higgins was appointed Enclosure Commissioner and he in turn even-handedly nominated solicitors from the town's two principal firms, Henry Bourne and Henry Wilson, as his Clerks, cautiously stipulating that it would be 'upon this principle nevertheless that in their charges.....there shall be a charge for only one Clerk although both may happen to be in attendance at one and the same time'. He also appointed Titus Bourne as his banker under the Act.

> ALFORD INCLOSURE.
>
> WE, the undersigned Proprietors of, or persons interested in, the Open and Common Arable Fields, and Open and Common Meadow or Pasture Lands and Fields, situate within the parish of Alford, in the county of Lincoln, do, by this notice under our hands, call a PUBLIC MEETING of the Proprietors and persons interested in the said Open and Common Arable, Meadow, and Pasture Lands and Fields, to be held at the WIND MILL INN in ALFORD aforesaid, on TUESDAY the Third day of OCTOBER next, at Eleven o'clock in the Forenoon, for the purpose of taking into consideration the expediency of inclosing the said Open and Common Arable, Meadow, and Pasture Lands and Fields, and of extinguishing all Right of Intercommonage (if any) which may exist over or in respect of such Lands, under the powers and provisions of an Act passed in the 6th and 7th years of the reign of his late Majesty King William the Fourth, intituled, "An Act for facilitating the "Inclosure of Open and Arable Fields in England and "Wales."—Given under our hands this thirteenth day of September, 1837.
> R. A. CHRISTOPHER.
> JOHN MAWER.
> JOHN TAYLOR, for himself and FRANCES TAYLOR.
> SAMUEL STEPHENSON.

54. Statutory advertisement in 1837 in anticipation of the Common Fields being enclosed. The local Conservative M.P., R.A. Christopher, was the principal owner of common land and the advertising was given to the Tory-supporting Lincolnshire Chronicle rather than Lincolnshire's principal newspaper, the liberal Stamford Mercury

In practice Bourne's office dealt with the legal business. As required by the Act, Henry Bourne or one of the managing clerks pinned the necessary formal notices on the church door and there were appropriate advertisements in the local press. Higgins then proceeded under his statutory powers allotting the land and setting out the routes of public and private roads and footpaths over the old fields.

When the Alford Enclosure Award was made, the process of open field enclosure over the country as a whole was already virtually complete. There was indeed a further General Enclosure Act of 1845 but this was designed to stimulate the enclosure of rough pasture commons, which in certain areas still survived.

Although, to opponents like Robert Sanderson or William Cobbett, enclosures and engrossers had destroyed England's landed peasantry and created beggars by lowering the agricultural workers standard of living, enclosure was perhaps an inevitable process and Alford probably had the most painless way of dealing with it, with the making of the Award and the final physical allotments only really recognising the natural engrossments of landholding that had taken place, almost imperceptibly, over the years.

Land Drainage

L and drainage has always been an important matter in the lowlands of Eastern England and especially so in the area of marshland between Alford and the North Sea. Commissioners for Sewers had been appointed

THE ALFORD CLERKSHIP TO THE LOCAL COMMISSIONERS OF SEWERS.

DEAR SIR,

We, the undersigned, being Commissioners regularly sitting at the Alford Court of Sewers, ask you to support the principle of a Local Clerk for the Local Court.

The three appointments of Spilsby, Louth, and Alford are advertised in the Stamford Mercury as quite distinct, and the elections are upon separate dates.

That for Alford is on Saturday next, the 2nd April, at the Sessions House, Alford, at eleven o'clock a.m.

We ask you therefore to support the principle shown above, of a local man being appointed as Clerk to the Local Court, and trust that you will make it convenient to attend at the time and place above-named.

Yours truly,

J. W. DAVY,
Great Carlton, Louth.

WM. HOFF,
Grebby Hall, Spilsby.

G. J. BROWN,
Tothby Manor, Alford.

J. N. ROBINSON,
Anderby Grange, Alford.

29th March, 1910.

55. Public appeal by local landowners in support of S.B. Carnley's candidature for the clerkship of the Alford Court of Sewers

by the Crown, in the same way as magistrates, since medieval times. Each ancient Anglo-Saxon wapentake had its own commissioners who held Courts of Sewers and appointed dikereeves to see to the operation of drains and sluices. The commissioners were generally local farmers.

The clerkship to the local Court of Sewers was a valuable appointment for local solicitors. But, although Alford had its own Court for the local wapentake of Calceworth, the clerkships for this and other local Sewer Courts were traditionally held by the old-established solicitors' firm of Walker & Co at the neighbouring market town of Spilsby.

In 1910 S.B. Carnley, with the support of local sewer commissioners, attempted to wrest the clerkship from the Spilsby solicitors by forcing an election for the post upon the principle that there should be 'a Local Clerk for the Local Court'. Commissioners from all over the county were entitled to vote in the Alford election. Arrangements had to be made for transporting promised supporters to Alford on election day and also for lunching them as an inducement to vote. Carnley booked for 40 lunches at Alford's White Horse Hotel but the Windmill Hotel was booked by Walkers for 60. And, in a close vote, his opponents' conservative argument that the clerkships had always gone together prevailed.

Commissioners of Sewers were abolished by the 1930 Land Drainage Act and the clerkship of the new Alford Drainage Board eventually came at last to the town, John Tinn taking over as clerk in 1950 and continuing in the post until 1970 when the Board appointed its own first full-time clerk.

The Corn Exchange

Alford's Corn Exchange was built in 1856 on a site given by the Lord of the Manor, R.A. Christopher. Its primary use was, of course, on Market Days, when corn merchants would be at their stands and farmers would meet up with them for trade but, as with most Victorian Corn Exchanges, the large trading floor was also hired out for public meetings and entertainments. And office rooms were also let out from time to time to business tenants. During both World Wars, the catering facilities at the Corn Exchange were requisitioned by the military authorities.

The Alford Corn Exchange Company Limited to which the Corn Exchange belonged was well supported throughout its existence. Frederick Rhodes (initially, jointly with L.J. Brackenbury) was the Company Secretary

56. Alford's Corn Exchange, used as such until the 1970s

and Bourne Rhodes & Co were formally appointed, on the Company's formation, as its bankers.

In 1889 Rhodes retired as a result of ill-health, having given 33 years' service as a Company Secretary, apparently on a voluntary basis, and Carnley was appointed to replace him with a salary of £5 per year. In his time, Carnley was always by far the largest shareholder of the Company and all Annual General Meetings and Meetings of the Directors seem to have been held at his office rather than in the Corn Exchange itself. At these meetings, Carnley appears always to have had a fistful of proxy votes available for use if required.

In 1947 the Company decided to accept an offer of £1,750, which had been made for the Corn Exchange by Alford Urban District Council, Carnley's having been the lone voice among the Directors opposing the sale. The sale proceeds were then paid out to the shareholders on the liquidation of the Company.

For a further 20 years or so the Council continued to have the building used for corn dealings on Tuesday Market Days.

Alford and District Traders' and Farmers' Association

This was formed at the instigation of S.B. Carnley in 1904. The Association generally had a membership of about 100 shopkeepers, farmers and other businessmen, drawn not only from Alford but also from the surrounding area. It enthusiastically promoted the interests of the town.

ALFORD SPOTTING COMPETITION.

16th NOVEMBER, 1935 to 23rd NOVEMBER, 1935.

In each of the windows belonging to the undermentioned Tradesmen will be found AN ARTICLE NOT SOLD BY THEM. This does not include their customary Fixtures, Fittings and Window Decorations.

CAN YOU SPOT THEM?

PRIZES will be given for the Forms returned containing the largest number of correct answers.

1st PRIZE 15/-   2nd 10/-   3rd 7/6   4th 5/-   5th 3/6   6th 2/6

All in the form of Vouchers, to be spent at undermentioned shops.

Completed Entry Forms to be left at the office of Messrs. PARKER & PORTER, Market Place, ALFORD, not later than 12 noon on MONDAY, November 25th, 1935.

	NAME OF TRADESMAN.		WHAT IT IS.
1	Allett, Miss Confectioner Market Place	/	Pencil Sharpener
2	Badley, W. Ironmonger ,,	2|	Three first aid sets
3	Stead & Simpson Boot Dealers ,,	1|6	Rexall Razor Blade
4	Chandler, E. T. Tailor West Street	/	Reel white cotton
5	Coney, R. Tailors & Outfitters Market Place	/	Fountain pen
6	Cooke Bros. Drapers West Street	2|	Key on string
7	Dawson, Z. E. Sadler Church Street	1|-	Manicure file
8	Dunn, C. A. Stationer Market Place	2|-	Taper holder
9	Evison, G. Grocer ,,	1|-	Manicure file
10	Gibbons, G. & Son Furnishers West St.	/	Needle case
11	Graves, F. Music Dealer ,,	1|-	White shoe button
12	Heely, F. W. Chemist ,,	2|6	Split ring
13	Hood, Miss Clothier Church St.	1|-	Safety Pin
14	Kemp, S. R. Chemist Market Place	2|6	CORK SCREW
15	Lingard, G. H. Plumber etc West St.	/	Cow and Gate Milk
16	Myers, C. W. Miller & Baker ,,	/	SUGAR LUMPS
17	Moore, H. H. Confectioner ,,	/	TOILET ROLL
18	Pridmore, W. E. E. & Co Clothiers ,,	1|-	KNITTING NEEDLE
19	Vickers & Porter, Fruiterers Church St.	/	½ Size Whiskey Bottle
20	Pycock, A. E. Baker South Street	/	KRUSCHEN SALTS
21	Rhodes, J. H. Boot Dealer West St.	2|-	SHARP'S SEWING NEEDLES
22	Stones, J. E. Ironmonger Market Place	2|-	QUIKK INK
23	Skinner, Mrs. Milliner South Street	/	JAR VANISHING CREAM
24	Summers, W. E. Grocer ,,	/	PEN KNIFE
25	Smith. A. Grocer ,,	/	SPOON
26	Smith, H. Boot Dealer West St.	/	2 WHITE HANDKERCHIEVES
27	Parker & Co. Butchers Market Place	2|-	POT EGG
28	Temple, F. Wireless Dealer ,,	2|6	POST CARDS
29	Watson, B. Pork Butcher West St.	1|-	BOTTLE SALTS
30	Wakelin J. Tobacconist Market Place	1|-	MAYNARDS CHOCOLATE CIGARETTE
31	Willey, F. Cycle Dealer West St.	/	PACKET DARNING NEEDLES

DUNN PRINTER ALFORD.

57. Spotting Competition organised by the Traders' Association in 1935

Transport links by train and bus were encouraged and the Association's own local timetables published. Local businesses were advertised in various ways and steps taken whenever possible to protect them from what was regarded as unfair competition from the larger stores and multiple shops establishing themselves in the early years of the century in the larger towns. Agreed opening hours and public holiday periods were fixed, advertised and required to be observed by all members. And the local MP was lobbied about the concerns of Alford people, for example, in 1904, 'for reduction of the speed limit from 20mph to 12mph' and 'for more stringent measures of terms of imprisonment for first offenders without the option of a fine, the last named being absolutely useless'. Carnley, as the Association's solicitor, was expected to keep its members abreast of new developments in the Law which might affect their businesses, and also give free general advice as to debt collection methods.

The Annual Dinners of the Association were always immensely popular. They were generally held at the White Horse and the tickets, limited to 80 for reasons of space, were invariably almost all snapped up by the members themselves. After the meal and speeches, entertainment was provided by two or three professional entertainers or musicians. This, Carnley often averred, was always 'looked forward to as the best musical entertainment of the year in this immediate neighbourhood.' He took great pains in selecting the performers and in briefing them as to what would be required and it is clear from his papers that there was a great deal of sentimentality in the communal entertainments of pre-wireless days. 'Our people are extremely fond of the old ballad songs', singers were told, 'and others more modern provided they have the necessary lilt of swing', while violinists were asked for 'a good and varied selection of all the Irish and Scotch airs'. Appropriately enough, the evenings were rounded off by community singing of the old songs which the visiting entertainers were expected to lead 'to go with a vim'.

Alford Bull Fair

A s long ago as the early 1700s the area of Lincolnshire around Alford had been famous for its red cattle. Daniel Defoe, making a tour of the area then, said it was remarkable that 'all the cows for fifty miles together were red or pyed red and white'. By the end of the eighteenth century cattle breeders in Lindsey Marsh were trying to improve their shorthorn herds. And scientific methods of breeding cattle, developing over the next century, resulted in Lincoln Red Shorthorns becoming a registered variety with a herd book of its own.

In 1901 S.B. Carnley, then in his energetic prime, took steps to have a Bull Fair established at Alford on a formal basis. Alford fair itself was probably of earlier origin than any other of its kind in Lincolnshire and Carnley was anxious to capitalise on the town's very advantageous location right in

ALFORD   BULL   FAIR

TUESDAY 7th NOVEMBER, 1905.

PURE RED SHORTHORN BREEDERS
PLEASE NOTE.

As previously advertised, PRIZES will be offered
for competition at the above important Fair, the
animals so competing in all cases to be actually and
bona-fide Sold in the Sale-ring to entitle them to the
Prize, and to be confined to Red Shorthorns, either
Registered or eligible for Registration in the respective Herd Books.

Seven Classes for BULLS, COWS, and HEIFERS,
including CHAMPION PRIZE of £20.

TOTAL PRIZE MONEY — £50.

Judges :
Peter Dunn, Esq., Sigglesthorne, near Hull—Bulls
not exceeding 15 months old.
John Evens, Esq., Burton, near Lincoln—Bulls over
15 months, females, and milkers.
Both Judges will combine in Class 7.
Entry Forms may now be obtained upon applica-
tion from the Chairman and the Auctioneers.
ENTRIES CLOSE at 4 p.m. on TUESDAY, 17th
OCTOBER, 1905.

A PUBLIC DINNER, limited to 140 Seats (nearly
120 are already booked), to be allotted strictly in order
of application, will be held on TUESDAY, 7th NOVEM-
BER, 1905, at 5.30 p.m., in the Corn-exchange in
Alford, when his Grace the DUKE of PORTLAND will
preside, and will be supported by the Right Hon.
Ailwyn E. Fellowes, Minister of Agriculture, the Right
Hon. Lord Heneage, Lord Willoughby de Eresby,
M.P., and several other influential Gentlemen.
Tickets, at 5s. each, may be purchased on or before
Tuesday, 17th October, 1905, ONLY from Brittan
Wakelin, stationer, Alford. No reservation of seats
will be made unless payment is made at time of
booking.
Further details and particulars may be obtained
from   S. B. CARNLEY,
                    Chairman of the Committee.
Alford, 25th September, 1905.

58. An advertisement in 1905 for the successful
Bull Fair

the home of the Lincolnshire Reds. So, as he characteristically put it, 'we aroused ourselves and took a thorough grasp of the situation.' And already in 1904 he was able to say that 'whereas in times past we only had a few bulls put into the ring, we now have hundreds.' 'Our Fair is flourishing exceedingly', he said and he went on to hope that one outcome of this would be the establishment at Alford of a proper Cattle Market.

The Alford Bull Fair was, as a local newspaper report in 1943 had it, 'one of the most successful ventures ever in the town.' In its early days a special Bull Fair Clerk was employed by Carnley at his office to run it. And its success inspired the foundation of the Cattle Market Company. The annual Bull Fair continued to be held at Alford until 1986 when it was transferred to the Lincolnshire Showground.

The Cattle Market

For more than seven centuries Alford has been a Market Town. Originally it had had Fairs on Whit Tuesday and 8th November each year but in 1867 three new Summer Fairs for livestock were started. And, from time immemorial, a weekly market had been held with tolls and stallages paid to the Lord of the Manor.

The cattle sales in the South Market Place were the subject of frequent complaints to the manorial courts of obstruction and nuisance and the lack of a proper market resulted in sales being lost to the nearby towns of Louth and Spilsby. So, stimulated by the success of the Bull Fair, the Alford Traders' and Farmers' Association were ready by 1912 to make Carnley's brainchild of a proper market in Alford a reality.

60. The Cattle Market shortly after its construction on 1912

ALFORD,

22nd March, 1911.

Dear Sir,

ALFORD STOCK MARKET.

It has been decided to form a STOCK MARKET FOR ALFORD AND DISTRICT, and to hold a Public Meeting in the Corn Exchange here on TUESDAY, 4th APRIL, 1911, at 3 p.m.

CAPT. A. G. WEIGALL, M.P., has promised to attend.

We hope you will be able to be present, and that the movement will have your practical support.

Yours faithfully,

S. B. CARNLEY, President,

THOS. B. PARKER, Vice-President,

T. NEALE, Secretary,

Alford and District Tradesmen's Association.

59. The genesis of the new Alford Cattle Market in 1911

The previous year the Alford Market Company Limited had been formed to lease the 'live tolls' from the Lady of the Manor and the new cattle market the Company set up in East Street was of the most modern kind. Its steel and cast-iron cattle pens were far superior to the wooden pens of older local cattle markets and the convenient Tuesday Market day made it popular with local auctioneers, farmers and butchers. In 1955, with substantial additional capital being required for modernization, the cattle market was sold to Alford Urban District Council, the Market Company being wound up afterwards. In 1960 the Council purchased the right to the livestock tolls and, after the local Council's own demise in 1974, the cattle market continued to be important in the town until it was closed in 1987 by East Lindsey District Council.

CHAPTER SIX
LAW AND ORDER

The Association for the Prosecution of Felons

Around the time of the Napoleonic Wars country areas such as Lincolnshire were experiencing a great deal of lawlessness. There

4 Guineas
REWARD.

Stolen

On the evening of Monday the 13th or early on the morning of Tuesday the 14th instant, from the Premises of Mr. JOHN TAYLOR, of WELL,

Two Hives of Bees.

Whoever will give such information as may lead to the conviction of the offender or offenders, shall on such conviction receive a reward of 3 GUINEAS from the Treasurer of the Alford Association for prosecuting Felons, and a further reward of 1 GUINEA from the said Mr. Taylor.

By Order,

Bourne and Carnley,

Secretaries to the said Association.

Alford, 15th Octr. 1817.

61. In 1817 the rewards offered to informants were comparable to a farm worker's annual wage

75

were several reasons for this but, sadly, the root cause was the extreme poverty of labouring people, whose hunger sometimes drove them to steal. The position was, however, exacerbated by migrant workers coming into the county for the building of the new transport links and by revolutionary ideas stemming from events in France. Violence sometimes erupted. There were riots in several East Lincolnshire market towns and arson attacks on farms. And in Alford demands for money were made of local tradesmen.

Law enforcement at the time still depended on unpaid Parish Constables, accountable through High Constables to the magistrates. The system was hopelessly inadequate and in every town alarmed country gentry, farmers and shopkeepers banded together in Associations for the Prosecution of Felons to offer rewards for help with convictions. These rewards were high, in respect of thefts typically around £5, the equivalent of the annual wage of an agricultural labourer at that time, and punishment for convicted offenders was severe, imprisonment or transportation for theft and the death penalty for arsonists.

The Associations for the Prosecution of Felons were very well supported. William Carnley was Secretary to the Alford Association and in 1796 he was able to announce 'the Fund is now considerable and the Subscribers at present don't think it expedient to pay any further annual Subscriptions; but such other Persons as chuse to become Members of this Association may at any Time be admitted upon Payment of 10s 6d into the Hands of the Treasurer'. Regular meetings were held in local hostelries. They appear to have been convivial and Carnley's newspaper advertisements were particularly designed to stress 'Dinner to be on the table at one o'clock' following the morning meetings.

Over the first half of the nineteenth century rural poverty gradually became rather less severe and at the same time measures were being taken to ensure law and order, culminating in the County and Borough Police Act of 1856 under which a proper police force had to be set up in the county.

The Alford Court of Requests

Courts of Request were the predecessors of the County Courts. They were set up in the seventeenth and eighteenth centuries under special Acts of Parliament covering different parts of the country. The Act setting up the Court for the Alford area was passed in 1780 and renewed in 1807.

62. From the record of the last meeting of Alford's Court of Requests 1847

The local Court consisted of approximately a dozen prominent members of the community appointed as Commissioners together with their lawyer-Clerk and a Court Serjeant, and its regular monthly hearings seem to have been held at the local hostelries.

The Courts dealt with claims for the recovery of small debts, their jurisdiction being limited to claims not exceeding £5. In Alford, the business of the Court seems to have been conducted efficiently and effectively. Quite often cases listed for hearing had been settled beforehand and Court orders frequently allowed for the repayment of debts by instalments. But retribution was severe if payments under a Court Order were not kept up, imprisonment being the sanction in such cases.

William Carnley had the Court Clerkship. So securely indeed did he hold the position that, when the Commissioners appointed Titus Bourne to succeed him on his death in 1806, Bourne had to undertake to pay the profits arising from the appointment to his widow, Elizabeth, during the minority of her 16-year-old son, William, and thereafter to share the profits equally with the son, on the assumption that he would in due course be appointed Joint-Clerk. Within a year, however, Mrs Elizabeth Carnley had rather blotted her copybook. The new Act of 1807 was anticipated and Mrs Carnley, in response to the appeal which went out for subscriptions to fund it, 'had not been so liberal as she ought according to the benefit which she derives under the present Act'. She therefore had her subscription money returned to her with a request to 'reconsider the Circumstances and make such further or other subscriptions as she shall think proper'. And by 1808 the unpopular Mrs Carnley had left the town. As things turned out, Titus Bourne became within a few years the sole Clerk, and continued, latterly with his own son Henry, running the Court for the remainder of its existence.

The County Courts Act of 1846 provided for the abolition of the Courts of Request, although the new County Courts which superseded them were founded on the same principles. There was no County Court for Alford, however, and the town has, since 1847, never had a civil court of law of its own.

CHAPTER SEVEN
TRANSPORT

Turnpike Roads and the Mail

Over the course of the eighteenth century communications throughout England were greatly improved. The traditional system by which parish councils had to look after the roads in their areas was no longer able to cope. Instead it became possible to obtain a special Act of Parliament by which a stretch of road was taken over by a local Turnpike Trust. Finance for maintaining and improving their stretch of turnpike was raised by the trustees from subscribers or by borrowing. And toll bars were erected at

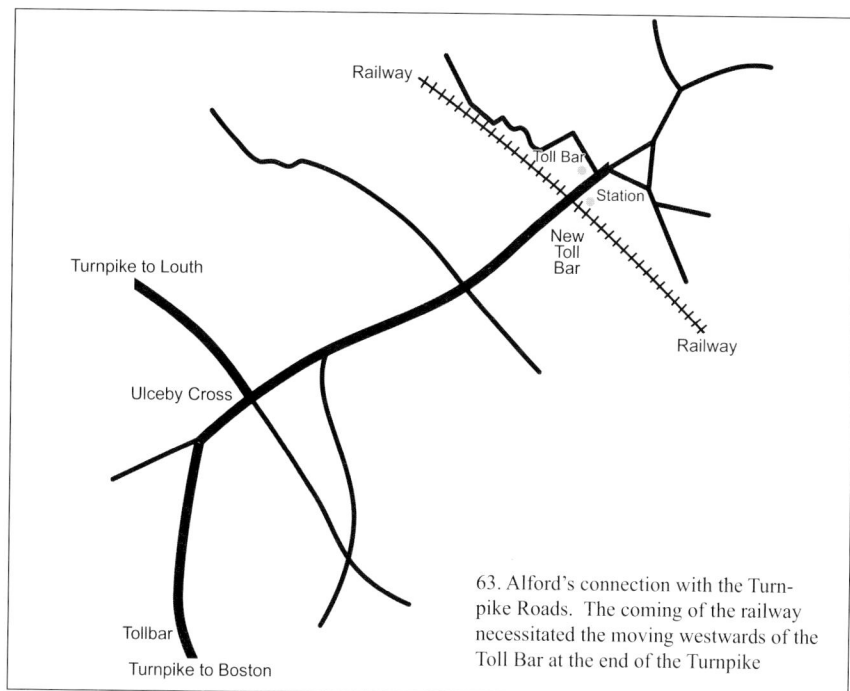

Railway

Toll Bar

Station

New Toll Bar

Turnpike to Louth

Railway

Ulceby Cross

Tollbar

Turnpike to Boston

63. Alford's connection with the Turnpike Roads. The coming of the railway necessitated the moving westwards of the Toll Bar at the end of the Turnpike

either end of the turnpike and at intermediate stages to enable charges to be recovered for the use of the road.

The turnpike system was comparatively late in coming to Lincolnshire. But in 1765 parliamentary approval was obtained for a turnpike to run between Alford and Boston. £8,125 was raised to finance it. The right to collect tolls on the road was then let by auction for successive periods of three years and the undertaking seems to have been economically sound.

As it turned out, Alford was effectively at the end of a spur running from the main road at Ulceby Cross, as a further Turnpike Trust operated from Louth to connect up with the Boston turnpike some three or four miles south of Alford to form a Boston-Louth-Grimsby trunk road link. And it was solicitors in Boston and Louth who obtained the direct advantages of acting for the two Turnpike Trusts and managing their business affairs.

64. Turnpike toll being collected at Toll Bar Cottage

The new turnpikes brought benefits to the area in many ways. Competing stagecoaches came up regularly from London to Boston and beyond and the journey up from London no longer had to be dreaded. In the early nineteenth century, a Royal Mail service started operating from London on the turnpikes through Boston to Louth and a mail cart from Alford went up every morning to the inn at the Ulceby turnpike junction to despatch the mail and returned each afternoon to collect the incoming mail. Titus

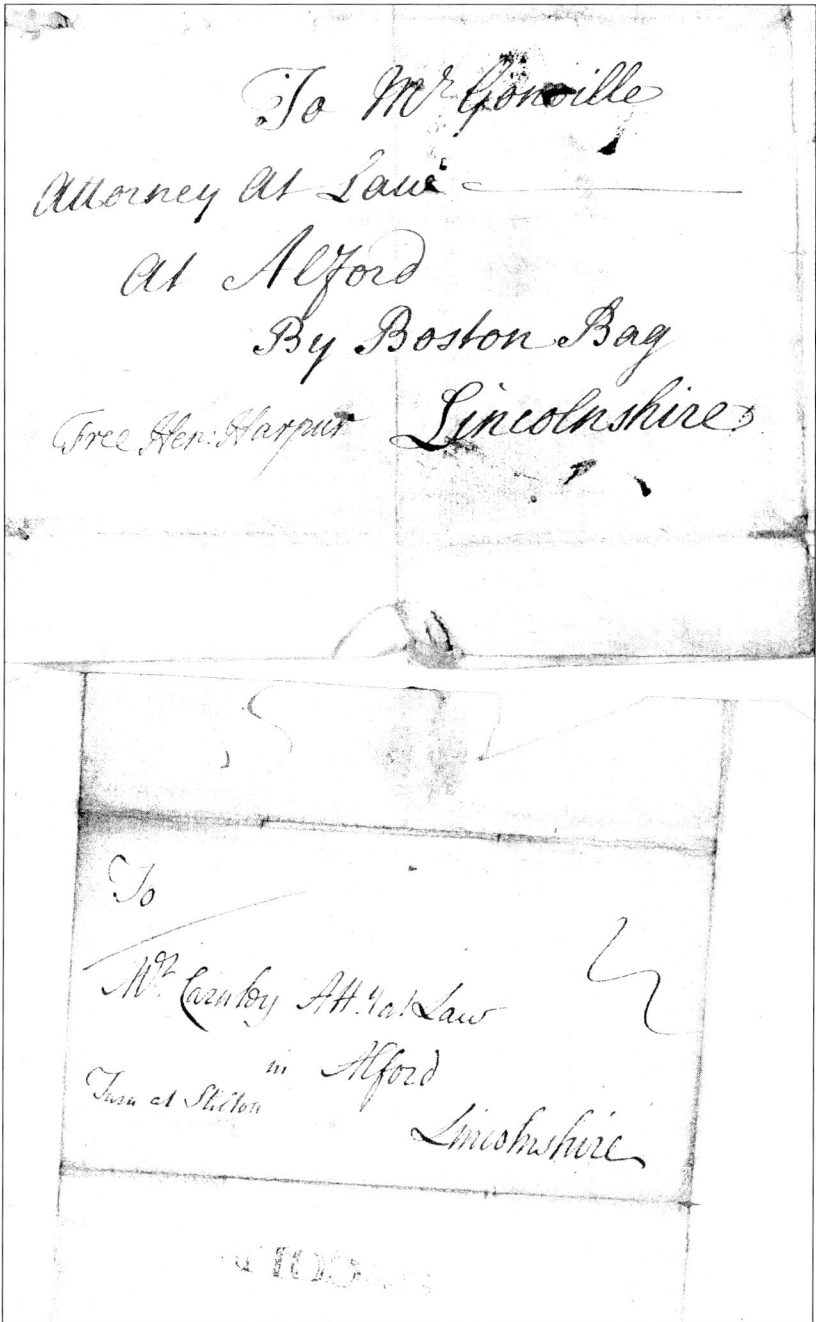

65. 18th century letters sent by stagecoaches on the turnpike roads and including directions of the kind required before the commencement of the Penny Post in 1840. The letter from London (above) travels in the Boston Bag and the letter from Lincoln (below) has to go by way of the important stagecoach junction at Stilton in Huntingdonshire.

Bourne's office in these days seems to have acted informally as the Post Office for the town.

Journey times on the turnpikes were dramatically cut, especially with the introduction of macadamised roads, and in the 1820s and 1830s turnpikes were at their peak. Their days were, however, numbered with the coming of the railways, although Alford's toll bar did actually remain in use for 20 years after the railway's arrival in the town. And the Alford historian R.C. Dudding, writing in 1930, could 'still remember the unwelcome halt on a cold winter day, fumbling for coppers, the cautious approach of the old man or woman who collected the toll, and the slow opening of the gate.'

Canals

The great age of canal building in England lasted from around 1760 to about 1830. Canal projects required private bill legislation and eventually conveyancing for land purchases along the canal's route. These were sources of substantial fees for solicitors. And speculation in canal company shares was also common in the boom years before the arrival of the railways.

Interest in canal building extended to Lincolnshire, though many of the canals proposed for the county never actually materialised. Samuel Johnson's friend Bennet Langton, who lived a few miles south of Alford, is mentioned in Boswell's Life of Johnson as having been much taken up with canal planning for the area in 1765. His canal was to have run through to Trusthorpe and Mablethorpe. A later plan was for there to be a canal from Alford to Wainfleet Harbour. But the most extensive efforts were made in 1825-26 when an Act of Parliament was obtained for a 5 mile long canal to be made between Alford and Anderby Creek near Skegness at an estimated cost of £43,000.

Titus Bourne was appointed Treasurer to the Alford Canal Company, his junior partner William Carnley also being on the Company's management committee, and these two were, jointly with the other local lawyer Henry Wilson, the solicitors who promoted the scheme. Their prospectus pointed out that 'notwithstanding the improved condition of Agriculture in the County of Lincoln there is at present no available outlet by the sea for the produce of the country between the Humber at Tetney and Boston Haven, a distance of nearly 60 miles'. And they drew attention to Thomas Telford 'the most eminent Engineer of the present day' having approved the detailed plans drawn up by the Company's own very experienced engineer Tierney Clark.

Copy of the first Document.

ALFORD NAVIGATION.

Having examined the Map and Section of the proposed Navigation, and perused the Report of the Engineer Mr. Tierney Clark, as well as several communications from the promoters of the measure, and had verbal explanations from Mr. Clark, as to the nature of the Ground through which the Canal will be excavated, and of the Sea Shore on which the Work will terminate ; I am of opinion that the Canal and back Drains have been judiciously laid out to answer the intended purposes, and as the Soil is said to consist chiefly of firm Clay, and as by the Sections no great height of embanking is required, there does not seem the least reason to doubt the practicability and stability of the work proposed to be performed, and as the Shore is also said to consist of firm Clay, it is favourable for the construction of protecting Jetties, in such direction as experienced Seamen shall recommend ; excavation for an entrance-basin in the before-mentioned Clay is likewise a favourable circumstance, but the dimensions of that Basin must of course be determined by the purposes for which it is intended.

By judicious management in the admission and discharge of tidal Water, the Basin and Entrance may be preserved of sufficient capacity.

THOS. TELFORD.

London, 24th November 1825.

66. Thomas Telford's endorsement of the plans of Alford Canal

By desire of the Committee for the Alford Canal, we beg leave to send you the annexed resolutions, and to solicit your interest and assistance. By those resolutions it will be seen when the next General Meeting is fixed, and at that Meeting we take the liberty of requesting your attendance.

H. WILSON,
T. BOURNE,   *Solicitors.*
W. CARNLEY,

Alford, 16th January 1826

☞ The hour of meeting will be at Eleven o'clock in the forenoon, and at half after Two a Public Dinner will be provided.

67. Solicitors' notice

In the event, the plans for the canal appear to have been somewhat defective and a critical shareholder, Stephen Langton, obtained Telford's admission that he had acted too hastily in approving them. The necessary funding for the canal was not forthcoming and work on the ground had not commenced when in 1833 the time for completion under the 1826 Act expired. And just a few years afterwards the railways appeared.

However, although the Alford Canal itself was never constructed, the building intended to be an inn at the site of the proposed dock terminal at Alford was and still stands today, being locally known, in reference to the name of the unfortunate speculator, as Coates's Folly.

68. Coates's Folly, the proposed inn at the site of the projected canal terminal

Railways

Railway mania swept the whole country in the 1840s and solicitors played a central role in promoting plans for railway lines and in piloting through the necessary parliamentary bills which might put them into effect. Titus Bourne and his son Henry were quick to respond. In the summer of 1845, before any railway was actually operating in Lincolnshire, they were issuing a prospectus for a line from Lincoln to a proposed big new double-armed harbour at Wainfleet. The line's principal object was to tap the burgeoning industrial markets of the Midlands and the North of England. But Bourne & Son's prospectus also contained in

69. A train at Alford Station in Great Northern Railway's days

passing what is believed to be the very first reference to the potential as a holiday resort of Skegness, 'an old and celebrated watering place on the coast near Wainfleet'. In the event, the projected £500,000 cost of this Lincoln, Wainfleet Haven and Boston Railway proved over-ambitious and the railways did not reach Skegness until 1873.

As early as 1850 virtually all the main railway lines in Lincolnshire were already in place. Thereafter it was a matter of constructing branch lines and improved connections between existing routes. Shortly after Frederick Rhodes came to Alford, for example, his firm took another initiative in proposing a branch line to Spilsby. This 1859 proposal again did not materialise (though Spilsby was eventually reached by rail in 1865) but the very brief surviving correspondence probably shows very typically the initial steps for a solicitor to take in organising railway promotion. The major local landowner, Lord Willoughby, had first to be discreetly approached through his Agent as his support would be a pre-requisite for success. Next there was to be a Private Meeting of 'some of the more influential members of the Spilsby Community desiring to promote the scheme'. This then could lead to the public promotion of the scheme and the issuing of Prospectus and Subscription forms seeking financial backing.

Such forms were once again distributed in the 1880s by Rhodes & Carnley with a view to introducing a parliamentary Bill for a Midland and East Coast Railway. The line was to run from the existing system at Melton Mowbray to the port at Boston, giving it the opportunity to 'rise to greater

WILLOUGHBY CHURCH.

OPENING OF THE NEW ORGAN.

ON THURSDAY, OCTOBER 23, 1856,

TWO SERMONS

WILL (D.V.) BE PREACHED IN

WILLOUGHBY CHURCH,

That in the Morning by the

REV. F. C. MASSINGBERD, M.A.,

RECTOR OF SOUTH ORMSBY;

And that in the Afternoon by the

REV. EDWARD DU PRE, M.A.,

Incumbent of Temple Guiting, Gloucestershire.

Divine Service will commence at 11 o'clock in the Forenoon, and 3 o'clock in the Afternoon. A Collection will be made after each Service in aid of the Fund for defraying the expenses of the Organ.

Mr. HOYLAND, of Louth, will preside at the Organ, and the Gentlemen of the LOUTH and HOGSTHORPE CHOIRS have kindly promised their assistance.

. *All Trains on the Great Northern Railway (except the up night Mail Train) will stop at Willoughby on that day.*

70. In passing through things temporal the Victorians did not lose sight of the things eternal: King's Cross - Grimsby main line trains had to make special stops on the day Willoughby Church's new organ was opened

things', and then to skirt the coast 'running through the populous and rich root-growing district known as the Holland's Towns' and terminate at the popular new resort of Skegness with a branch to 'the charming little watering-place' of Chapel St. Leonards.

There were still flickers of enthusiasm for new railways at the beginning of the next century and as late as 1906 S.B. Carnley was approaching the Great Central Railway to see if they were interested in constructing a new railway to link Horncastle via Alford to the Coast.

The Alford and Sutton Tramway

In 1883-84 a single line steam tramway with a 2ft 6in gauge was constructed between Alford and Sutton-on-Sea at a cost of about £16,000. The seven-mile long tramway passed along the centre of the public highway and the Tramway Company had to maintain the roadway between the metals and for a distance of 9in on either side making in all 4 feet. There was no paving between the metals, except at crossroads or where there were points or doubled-line passing places for the tramcar. And so the construction of the line was vigorously opposed from the outset because of the obstruction it would cause to ordinary traffic.

Nevertheless the tramway got off to a good start. The streets of Alford were well-decorated for the festive opening on 2nd April 1884 and a large banner strung across the front of Rhodes & Carnley's office wished 'Success to the Alford and Sutton Tramway'. On Good Friday 11th April Frederick Rhodes noted in his diary that the Wesleyan Sunday School tea party was much less well-attended than usual by reason of the tramcar running extra journeys to Sutton with passengers and on the Easter Bank Holiday Monday he said 'the tram car to Sutton on the new tramway crowded with passengers all day'. Green's Lincolnshire Villages later reported, apparently with information supplied by S.B. Carnley, that 'every Tuesday and Saturday this tramway was well-patronised and brought passengers from afar'. And the tramway was also authorised to have wagons coupled with the tramcars to carry livestock, coal and coke and other merchandise.

As a result of the initial optimism it was planned to construct a second tramway from Skegness to join the Alford and Sutton Tramway at Bilsby. This would have involved a new tram depot at Chauntry House, on the site of Alford's old Grammar School. Some preliminary work was done for the proposed new depot but the work on the projected Bilsby - Skegness line itself was never started.

71. The workforce constructing the new tramway pictured outside the High Street premises in 1883. The young S.B. Carnley can be seen behind in the office doorway.

72. On the opening day in 1884 a banner across the outside of Carnley's office wished success to the new tramway

As solicitor to the Tramway Company, S.B. Carnley was characteristically ever-vigorous in its support but his papers show that even the early encouraging traffic returns were really only on a very small scale. And they never had a proper chance to develop. For, as Rhodes' diary ominously noted on 20th June 1884 'heard that Sutton Railway Bill had passed Committee of House of Lords'. When the railway line from Willoughby through Sutton to Mablethorpe opened in 1886 the tramway's traffic returns immediately collapsed. As R.C. Dudding's History of Alford unsympathetically remarks 'the line ran its ignominious course, not even paying its way, just long enough to prevent Alford from becoming the natural terminus of the Sutton railway'.

The tramway struggled on until its closure in 1889 and the Tramway Company then went into liquidation. Carnley, however, still remained enthusiastic about the actual tramway itself. He called a public meeting in Alford with a view to acquiring it 'lock stock and barrel' for the town. Preliminary approaches were made to the Vestries of the various parishes through which the tramway passed to obtain support for its continuing in being and the Company was prepared to sell everything, including the rolling stock and the shedding and depot at each end, for £500. The total construction costs, Carnley informed Green's Villages, were over £21,000 but at a second meeting he was instructed to offer a mere £200 which offer was refused, the assets being later purchased by a Newcastle firm and sold off for considerably more than £500. Many years later, when George Dow was writing his book on the Tramway and interviewed Carnley about the matter, Carnley's recollection was of £300 having been the rejected offer. George Dow may have been describing Carnley in saying 'another venerable resident saw me in his office wherein, on a blazing July morning, burned two candles and an incandescent gas lamp'. In any event, Dow found the 85-year-old Carnley still incandescent in his indignation at the opportunity he thought the town of Alford had missed.

CHAPTER EIGHT
Financial

Money Scrivening

There were no bankers as such in country towns before the end of the eighteenth century. Solicitors until then provided basic services for investors and borrowers. Clients' money was deposited with them in their normal course of business and they were better placed than anyone else locally to see good opportunities for investment. They were also a source of credit for local landowners and business people and money-scrivening was a most important part of a country solicitor's practice. This was particularly so as the century progressed and huge amounts of capital were required for redevelopment of the countryside.

William Carnley was typical of the successful country practitioners of his time. His advertisements in the local press headed 'Money wanted' sought large investments for farmer-clients wanting to mortgage their properties and at the same time indicated that his own office had "several small sums to lend land upon approved securi*y*".

Banking

Although the London banks with their Clearing House system were already well established by the middle of the eighteenth century, there were no banks in Lincolnshire until Garfit Claypon & Co (originally Garfit & Co) opened at Boston in 1754. Another bank opened in Lincoln in 1775 and numerous other banks opened up in the larger towns towards the end of the century. But it was really impossible for very strong banks to exist beyond London while there were restrictions, in favour of the Bank of England, prohibiting joint stock banking being carried on outside the capital.

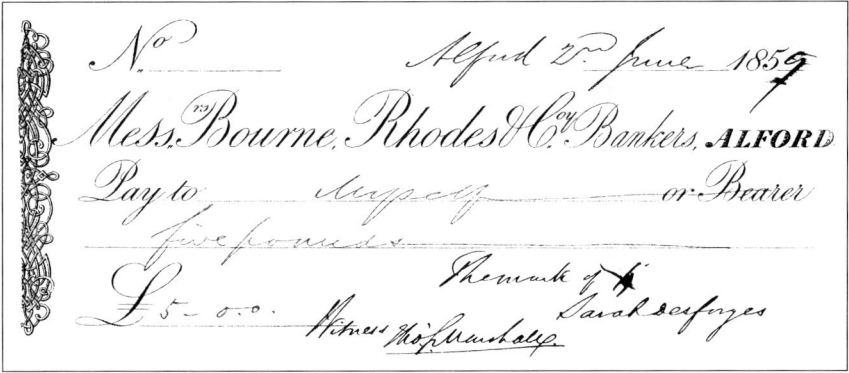

No

Alford 2nd June 1859

Mess. Bourne, Rhodes & Co. Bankers, **ALFORD**

Pay to   Myself   or Bearer

five pounds

£ 5 — 0.0.   Witness Tho. Marshall

The mark of ✗
Sarah Senfoyes

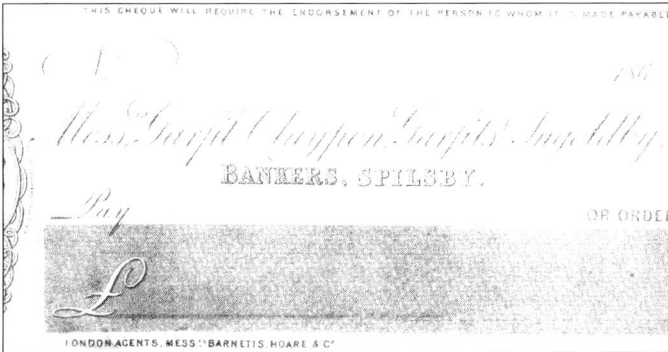

THIS CHEQUE WILL REQUIRE THE ENDORSEMENT OF THE PERSON TO WHOM IT IS MADE PAYABLE

Mess. Garfit Claypon Garfits Amcableby

BANKERS, SPILSBY.

Pay   OR ORDER

£

LONDON AGENTS, MESSRS BARNETTS, HOARE & CO

73. Private Bankers such as Bourne Rhodes & Co and Garfit Claypons gave way in the nineteenth century to joint stock banks… and the county based joint stock banks were themselves eventually taken over by banks operating on a nationwide scale

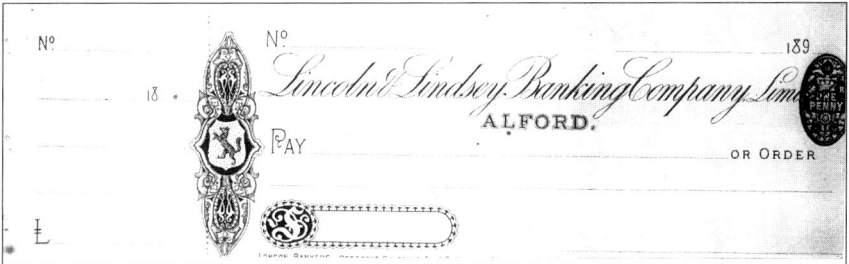

No   No   189

Lincoln & Lindsey Banking Company Limited
ALFORD.

PAY   OR ORDER

18

£

ONE PENNY

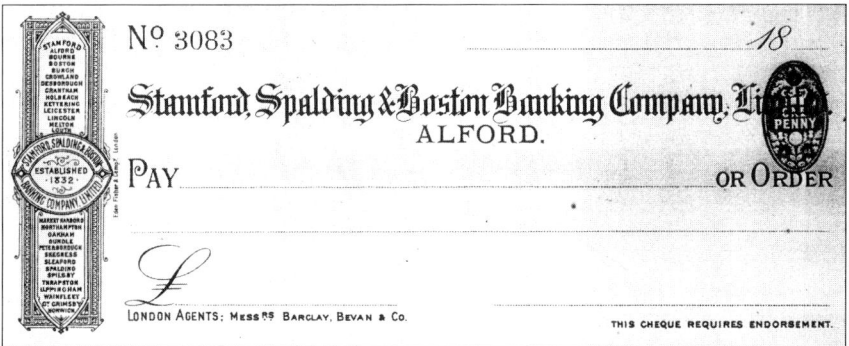

No 3083   18

Stamford, Spalding & Boston Banking Company, Limited.
ALFORD.

PAY   OR ORDER

£

LONDON AGENTS: MESSRS BARCLAY, BEVAN & CO.

ONE PENNY

THIS CHEQUE REQUIRES ENDORSEMENT.

The earliest banks in East Lincolnshire, such as Franklin Bourne and Franklin, were small private concerns run by minor gentry or prosperous land agents or solicitors. They were well-placed to help with the financing of drainage, enclosures, canals, turnpikes and other improvement works in the area. In normal times, private bankers generally found no difficulty in carrying on their business. They knew their customers and their customers knew and trusted them. Indeed, Richard Jefferies, writing in the late 1870s, remembered that the notes issued by the old banks were 'even preferred to the notes of the Bank of England, which at one time, in outlying country places, were looked on with distrust'. The financial strains of the Napoleonic Wars, however, led on to severe post-war economic conditions. Hazardous investments made during the booming early nineteenth century industrial expansion added to the difficulties and many private banks went under over this period.

As a result of the banking crisis, joint stock banking was allowed in the provinces. Two of the new joint stock banks, the Stamford Spalding and Boston Bank and the Lincoln and Lindsey Bank were Lincolnshire-based and, in a nationwide tendency, as the joint stocks banks established themselves, so the private bankers disappeared.

Titus Bourne's Alford Bank was developed and expanded in the teeth of the various crises which wore down other small country bankers. He established the banking business in 1822. But it was on too small a scale for outsiders really to be alive to it. The Lincoln & Lindsey Bank reconnoitred the area in 1834, before opening their agency at Alford, 'at which place' they reported, 'there is at present no regular Banking establishment'. Their new agency, conducted from a local ironmongers, and the weekly Tuesday market day attendance at Alford by Stamford Bank representatives from Spilsby produced competition Bourne seems easily to have been able to withstand. He enjoyed very high local credit and operated regular market day banking attendance at Spilsby. Occasional attendances were also made elsewhere, Rhodes's 1858 diary recording 'went with Mr. Bourne to Spilsby Market taking Mr. Marshall with us to Partney to attend to bank matters at the Sheep Fair'.

By the time official registration requirements for banks had become comprehensive, almost all the small country banks would have disappeared but Titus Bourne, swimming strongly against the tide, only appeared in national historical banking records for the first time in 1844. The little bank was in good health when Titus Bourne died in 1859. Lincolnshire's oldest bank, Garfit Claypon & Co, were continuing successfully as large private bankers and had been very supportive. In the event, Frederick Rhodes was unable to continue it and sold out to the Stamford Bank in 1862. Matthews and Tukes's History of Barclays Bank says of the purchase of Bourne Rhodes & Co that, in view of the 'small sum' of £534 representing gross profit, 'it may reasonably be assumed it was not quite in the front rank!'. However, as the Bank was operated as a sideline with negligible overheads, the net profit figure would presumably have been unusually high.

Alford continued to be served by the two Lincolnshire joint stock banks for some years after 1861. All the Lincolnshire banks were, however, very vulnerable when agriculture went into depression at the close of the century and by this time even the largest country based banks could no longer compete with the Clearing Banks from London.

Savings Banks and Building Societies

In the harsh economic conditions during and following the Napoleonic Wars not only was it very difficult for working people and small tradesmen to save but lawlessness and the absence of proper policing made it dangerous for savings hoards, however small, to be known to be kept at home. So the Trustee Savings Bank Act of 1817 enabled the small saver to deposit his money with local savings banks, supervised and run by entirely unpaid trustees, treasurers and managers, and to get a modest rate of interest on it.

Getting on for 200 local savings banks had been set up within a few months of

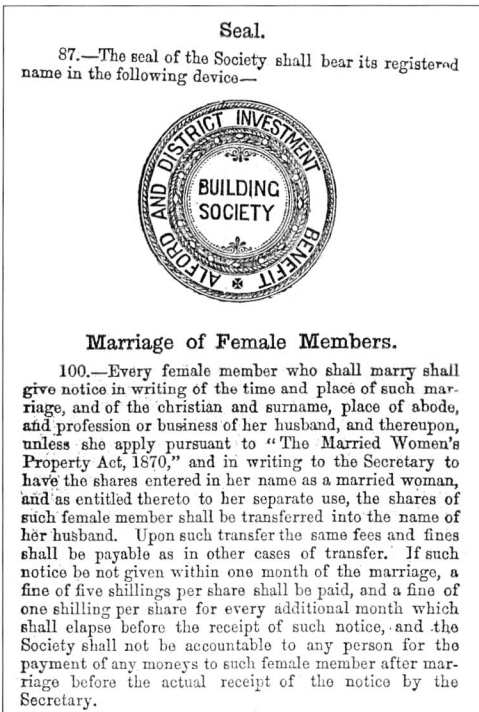

Seal.

87.—The seal of the Society shall bear its registered name in the following device—

ALFORD AND DISTRICT INVESTMENT BENEFIT BUILDING SOCIETY

Marriage of Female Members.

100.—Every female member who shall marry shall give notice in writing of the time and place of such marriage, and of the christian and surname, place of abode, and profession or business of her husband, and thereupon, unless she apply pursuant to "The Married Women's Property Act, 1870," and in writing to the Secretary to have the shares entered in her name as a married woman, and as entitled thereto to her separate use, the shares of such female member shall be transferred into the name of her husband. Upon such transfer the same fees and fines shall be payable as in other cases of transfer. If such notice be not given within one month of the marriage, a fine of five shillings per share shall be paid, and a fine of one shilling per share for every additional month which shall elapse before the receipt of such notice, and the Society shall not be accountable to any person for the payment of any moneys to such female member after marriage before the actual receipt of the notice by the Secretary.

74. Excerpts from the rules of Alford and District Building Society

the 1817 Act coming into force and, the movement being particularly popular in Lincolnshire, one of these was the Alford Savings Bank. Titus Bourne's managing clerks, William Sylvester and Thomas Marshall were successively its first Clerks and Actuaries and Frederick Rhodes eventually became its unpaid Treasurer and Managing Director. Like almost all contemporary savings banks it was on a very small and unambitious scale, only open between 7 and 8pm on Friday evenings in a shop in the Market Place.

With the establishment of the Post Office Savings Bank in 1861, local savings banks faced strong competition. There were a number of well-publicised failures in other parts of the country and even well-run local banks with their one day a week opening were unable to survive. When Parliament came to review the savings bank crisis in 1889, a very large number of the remaining little banks had had to give up business over the preceding 12 months. One of these was the savings bank at Alford, which had closed that very year. Two years later the 1891 Savings Bank Act finally set up the Trustee Savings Bank movement on a secure basis.

Further competition for the savings banks had come from the building societies. These, like Friendly Societies, had originated in the latter part of the eighteenth century but it was in the period after 1850 that the building society movement really began to take shape. The Alford and District Investment Benefit Building Society, founded in 1876, its roots having been in a local savings club, was able to take advantage of the demise of the local savings bank. Although itself operating on a very modest scale, it was efficiently run and continued in business for 80 years. Eventually, however, it was too small to survive and in 1956 Robert Hornby arranged for its merger into the Halifax Building Society whose local agency he had for some years been running in the town.

Friendly Societies

In the days before the Welfare State, people were largely responsible for looking after themselves in sickness, unemployment or old age and in the eighteenth century Friendly Societies began to grow up in which members could club together to insure themselves against misfortune.

The early Friendly Societies were generally purely local in character and not on a very well-organised basis. And as they usually met in public houses their members' money was often spent more on socialising than in

THE FORTY-SECOND ANNUAL REPORT
OF
THE LOYAL ALFORD LODGE
Grand United Order of Oddfellows,

Held at the   For the Year

RED LION HOTEL,   Ending December 31st,

East End, Alford.   **1904.**

Established July 25th, 1862.   Rules Registered September 24th, 1862.   Re-Registered as a Branch of the Grand United Order of Oddfellows, April 4th, 1882.

Rules Revised and Passed at a Special Summoned Lodge, held on March 19th, 1902, and Registered October 8th, 1902.

Honorary Members.

Mrs. Hamilton Ogilvy .. Biel, N.B	Rev. S E Nichols .. Alford	Mr. J. W. Chambers .. Alford
,, B. Wakelin .. Alford	J. W. Davy, Esq Great Carlton	,, T. A. Bellamy .. ,,
,, C. Birkett .. ,,	Frederick Higgins, Esq , J F. Alford	,, F. D. Lake .. ,,
,, S. Wheatley .. ,,	Rev. M. Riggall .. ,,	,, E. H. Young .. Beesby
Misses Dawson .. ,,	Dr. Dale (Medical Officer) .. ,,	,, R. Coney .. Alford
Miss Amy Kell .. ,,	T. N. Loy, Esq .. ,,	T. M. Winch, Esq. Legbourne Abbey
,, Edith Mary Kell .. ,,	Dr. Bosson .. ,,	S. W. Allinson, Esq. .. Alford
,, Mabel Grace Kell .. ,,	S. B. Carnley, Esq. (Solicitor) ..	G. J. Brown, Esq , c.c. Tothby House
Lord Willoughby de Eresby, M.P.,	C. O. Parr, Esq. .. Well	Dr. Sandall .. Alford
Grimsthorpe Castle	H. Budibent, Esq .. Rigsby	Mr. H. Christian .. ,,
Rev. C. W. Baron, M A. (Vicar) Alford	J. E. H. Sergeant, Esq. .. Alford	,, H. Walker .. ,,
Rev. M. S. Lawrence, (Curate) ,,	F. L. Walker, Esq. .. Spilsby	,, G. Boulton .. ,,
Rev. W. O. Massingberd, M.A., J F,	Messrs. Robinson Bros. .. Alford	,, T. Neale .. ,,
South Ormsby	Mr. G. Green .. ,,	,, J. Young .. ,,

TRUSTEES.

Mr. E. A. Young .. .. .. Park Lane

Bro. R. Thompson. | Bro. G. Curtis, P.G. | Bro. F. Allett, P.G. | Bro. R. C. Burgess, P.G.

MEDICAL OFFICER .. .. .. Dr Dale | SOLICITOR .. .. S. B. Carnley, Esq.

OFFICERS OF THE LODGE.

Bro H. J. Harpham Past Noble Grand	Bro. R. Garfit, P.G. .. Secretary	Bro. J. Sampson, P.G. Relieving Officer
,, J. R. Laine, .. Noble Grand	,, H. Fletcher, P.G. Assistant Sec.	,, R. C. Burgess, P.G. Sick Visitor
,, F. H. Ingamells Vice Grand	,, T. B Parker, P.G. Treasurer	

AUDITORS.

Bro. F. Allett, P.G. | Bro. G. Wakelin, P.G. | Bro. G. Curtis, .P.G.

Respected Brethren,—This Lodge is a branch of the Grand United Order of Oddfellows, and the Order is one of the oldest Friendly Societies in the World. Its objects are to aid the sick, comfort the mourners, and relieve the distressed. Its principles are founded upon the great precept : " Bear ye one another's burden "; also to be charitable in all things, to cultivate a benevolent spirit, and to teach men to provide against times of Sickness, Accidents, and Death.

It is very gratifying to your officers to find there has been 27 initiations, and one member accepted by clearance during the year, and as the success of a Lodge can only be secured and perpetuated by hearty co-operation, it is hoped that every member will take a lively interest in all that concerns its welfare, and endeavour to strengthen the ranks by proposing young and healthy candidates during the coming year ; the payments are easy, and the benefits are great.

We wish to direct attention to the great good this Lodge is doing. We find that over £230 has been paid to 81 Sick Members, and £128 in Death claims. It will be observed that although only £50 has been saved during the year, yet the Balance Sheet will show the sound financial position of the Lodge ; that after over 42 years experience, and paying all demands, the Lodge has saved the grand sum of £3408, thus proving that the small contributions paid by the members are equal to the large benefits offered. It may not be uninteresting to note that this Lodge was opened on July 25th, 1862, with 42 members, now over 42 years ago. 21 members have passed away, and their friends have received the funeral gifts from the Lodge. 13 left through non-payment. There are to-day 9 original members, including the founder of the Lodge.

The officers and members of the Lodge specially wish to record their thanks to the ladies and gentlemen whose names appear on on this report as Honorary Members, for their liberal support, and wishing all a happy and prosperous year,

We Remain, yours Respectfully and Fraternally,

H. J. HARPHAM, Past Noble Grand.

J. R. LAINE, Noble Grand.

F. H. INGAMELLS, Vice Grand.

T. B. PARKER, Treasurer.

R. GARFIT, Secretary.

E. WAKELIN, PRINTER, ALFORD.

75. Annual Report of the Oddfellows Friendly Society's Alford Lodge in 1904, the Lady of the Manor leading the list of Honorary Members from her "North British" address in Scotland

making provision for the future. But in the nineteenth century legislation of various kinds encouraged the growth of large Friendly Societies such as the Foresters and the Oddfellows which operated on a nationwide basis. These expected exemplary behaviour from their members and operated very much in the context of Christian religion. During the century they rapidly expanded their presence in Lincolnshire and by 1900 there were Friendly Society lodges or branches not only in country towns like Alford but also in the larger villages round about such as Burgh-le-Marsh, Withern and Aby.

Quite apart from their financial significance local Friendly Societies were important social institutions not only for their members but, with their annual celebrations and parades, throughout their local communities and they were particularly prominent at festivals for Coronations and Royal Jubilees.

Annual Friendly Society church services were usually held in parish churches and the clergy and other well-to-do local personages often made valuable contributions to funds by being Honorary Members. S.B. Carnley was very prominent as solicitor to a number of the local lodges.

Insurance

Fire Insurance really developed out of the disastrous consequences of the Great Fire of London in 1666. Insurance companies were originally on a very small scale. Each company had to provide its own fire-fighting service and, as a result, business had to be concentrated almost entirely in London. Some agencies with subsidised fire engines were established in the eighteenth century in provincial towns but it was quite impossible for insurers to attempt to support fire brigades on anything like a nationwide basis.

By the early nineteenth century, however, there was a huge demand

201st Year of the Office.

SUN FIRE OFFICE,
FOUNDED 1710.

The Oldest Insurance Office in the World.

Insurances effected on the following risks:—

FIRE DAMAGE.

RESULTANT LOSS OF RENT & PROFITS.

Employers' Liability and Workmen's Compensation, including Accidents to Domestic Servants.	Personal Accident, Sickness and Disease, Fidelity Guarantee, Burglary, Plate Glass.

HULL BRANCH, Lowgate.

H. W. JACKSON, Branch Manager

Local Agent:

Alford.—Mr. S. B. CARNLEY.

76. Sun Insurance advertisement in 1911

for insurance. Life assurance had by then developed on a scientific basis and local authorities followed London's example in setting up proper fire services under their own control. A whole new market for house insurance became evident all over the country and a host of new companies sprang up to meet the need.

The Sun (now merged into the Royal Sun Alliance group) was one of the early insurance companies with a history stretching back to the days of Queen Anne. In the early nineteenth century they greatly expanded their network of local agencies and concentrated particularly on having their agencies in solicitors' offices. By 1846 they had 677 agencies across the country and one of the Agents appointed in the Sun's expansionary drive was Bourne & Son's managing clerk, William Sylvester.

Insurance agencies in Alford were generally drawn from a very wide field. The other Law Office with an agency belonged to Robinson Farrow, who was described as 'Solicitor, Ironmonger and Agent for the Guardian Insurance Co'. Other Agents came from a range of occupations in shops and offices, several, like Farrow, combining roles which would nowadays be regarded as incongruous, Richard Burkitt being for example 'auctioneer and valuer, oilcake and manure merchant and insurance agent'.

Right up until almost the end of the twentieth century, the big insurance companies continued to have their own district offices, each with satellite agencies, able to give personal attention to their customers' requirements.

CHAPTER NINE
Education

The Grammar School

Alford Grammar School was founded in 1566, receiving its charter from Queen Elizabeth in 1576, and it soon became very much the focal point of the town. So much so that its governors had influence as a body, not just in school matters but in the general life of the town.

For the administration of the School's financial affairs the Governors needed to appoint one of their number each year to act as Bursar. This job was typical of so many in the administration of smaller country towns which were generally filled by local solicitors. So it was natural that successive principals of a firm should always have been on the governing body and prepared to keep the school's accounts and handle money on the Governors'

77. The Old Grammar School building at the junction of West Street and Chauntry Road in use prior to 1881

78 . The 1883 Grammar School premises not long after they were built

behalf. They seem indeed often to have been appointed almost as a matter of course and at a very young age. William Carnley Junior, for example, was elected Governor at only 21 years old and Titus Bourne, appointed at 23, went on to serve for what may perhaps be a record 53 years.

Education in the early nineteenth century was badly in need of reform and Grammar Schools generally were in a state of decline. Acts of Parliament in 1869 and 1870 were designed to remedy the position and the School Governors at Alford vigorously responded to the new climate. Frederick Rhodes, who in succession to Titus Bourne had almost invariably been elected Bursar each year to manage the School's business affairs, was closely involved in the radical reforms.

A thorough reorganisation of the School's constitution, finances and teaching curriculum was made in 1877 under a scheme of the Charity Commissioners. And in 1881 the School moved into new purpose-built premises on land where the subsequently expanded School still stands. Under the new 1877 constitution a Clerk to the Governors was to be appointed instead of the Governors electing one of their number as Bursar. Frederick Rhodes and Sidney Carnley were successively appointed as Clerks and meetings of the School Governors were generally held at their office.

On the death of Frederick Rhodes, Sidney Carnley had resigned his Governorship and became Clerk to the Governors instead. However the Governors were soon split between his supporters and those who disliked his style. In 1907 he managed to get his new young partner, Geoffrey

Staniland, appointed in his place but upon the acrimonious dissolution of the Carnley and Staniland partnership the following year, the Governors were not willing to reappoint Carnley to the clerkship. It was to be 1942 before the clerkship returned to his office with the appointment of Robert Hornby and he was eventually succeeded in 1968 by John Tinn.

Until the Butler Education Act of 1944, providing state finance for Grammar Schools, the Clerks to the Governors had a great deal of administrative work to do. They were responsible, through the Governors, for appointing headmasters and other school staff, supervising the school's finances and managing its buildings and its investments, payments for everything from the headmaster's salary to insignificant items of kitchen equipment being handled through the Clerk's own office.

The National Schools

In an expansion of education typical of what was happening all over the country, three new National Schools were founded in Alford during the course of the nineteenth century to supplement the Grammar School. National Schools were for practical purposes run by the Church of England, as opposed to the competing British Schools operating on a non-denominational but nevertheless firmly Christian basis.

The first of the new schools, built in 1820, provided Alford with teaching on a wide scale for the first time. The initiative for it had been taken by the Vicar at a Vestry Meeting. At the time the Vestry provided civil as well as ecclesiastical leadership in the town, as illustrated by the fact that Titus Bourne, a Wesleyan Methodist, as well as William Carnley Junior, was appointed with a third colleague to represent the Vestry in arranging with the Grammar School Governors for the setting up of the new school. The Governors also appointed three members to a six-man committee and Bourne and Carnley being, of course, themselves also Grammar School Governors, everything proceeded smoothly. The fundamentals were that the new school aimed to supply virtually free education for all local children, the education was to be on the principles of the Established Church and the children had to attend the Parish Church each Sunday (subject to exemption for the children of dissenters who could show Sunday attendance at their parents' place of worship) and that the school was to be regarded as 'an essential part' of the Grammar School which was to be responsible for its management and the appointment of its clergyman-teacher.

CORRESPONDENCE.

THE ALFORD PARLIAMENT AND THE LOCAL CHARITIES.

To the Editor of the Louth Advertiser.

Dear sir,—The *coup de grace* was, I imagine, effectively administered to the mischievous mal-contents, composing a certain section of the local legislators on Wednesday evening last—at any rate so far as the much debated subject of the Spendluffe Charity is concerned.

More than twelve months ago I pointed out how that body was stultifying itself by trying in effect to prove that the moon was made of green cheese, *e.g.*, that the Spendluffe Charity was within the all-reaching and powerful arm of the Council. That august body then, or, I should say, certain wiseacres upon it openly stated they were backed up by the so-called all powerful Charity Com-missioners, from whose opinion it was somewhat boastfully remarked by one member that there was no appeal, save to the Court of Appeal—thereby displaying his supreme ignorance of the rules of procedure. How well and how accurately he has guided his fellows, and how consternation was depicted upon the countenances of the would-be reformers when the Assistant Commissioner gave his opinion last Wednesday evening is better imagined than described. When, sir, will our Council enlist that best of all comrades into their debates—common sense—at present conspicuous only by its absence?

I enclose my card, and am yours, &c.,

FIAT JUSTITIA.

---

79. Carnley's unwisely premature letter to the Louth and North Lincolnshire's Advertiser's celebrat-ing the preliminary findings of the 1899 Public Enquiry which had supported his defence of the status quo regarding the National Schools.

In 1851 a wealthy local builder, John Rear, financed the establishment of a Girls' School and in 1865 a new Boys' School was built nearby, whereupon the old 1820 school was given up to the Infants.

All three schools operated on the same principles as National Schools and all three were subject to the authority of the Grammar School until 1877, when, with the reorganization of the Grammar School's constitution, the National Schools became independent. However, even before 1877, the most important role in managing the National Schools had always been played by the Vicar. This was partly because he was himself a Governor of the Grammar School, partly because he was Vicar with the importance of his post being emphasized in each of the National Schools constitutions and partly because he was chairman of the Vestry. Frederick Rhodes too, as Grammar School Bursar and later clerk of the Governors and acting for the Vicar in Vestry matters, was closely involved in the National Schools' affairs.

The National Schools operated successfully in their traditional manner and S.B. Carnley, writing in 1900, said 'it is generally admitted by all residents of this Town that the school under its present management could not be improved upon'. But by then the new Alford Urban District Council had come into existence under the 1894 Local Government Act and it was claiming the right under the 1894 Act to appoint trustees of the charity which underlay the National Schools' constitutions. Acting for the Vicar and Churchwardens, Carnley strongly resisted this claim, which the Council had only by a slim 7 to 5 majority resolved to pursue, and which he said was 'only the action of a few unruly spirits who wish to upturn every Institution of any standing'. He argued that the charity, being an ecclesiastical Charity and for Elementary Schools, was exempt from the 1894 Act.

The Council pursued their claim with the Charity Commissioners but the preliminary decision of their Assistant Commissioner at the Public Enquiry held at Alford in 1899 had been in Carnley's favour. Thereafter he had sent an unpleasantly arrogant crowing letter under a pseudonym to a local newspaper celebrating his position. But the Charity Commissioners eventually went against their own preliminary findings and backed the Council. Carnley fought on, taking both them and the Council to the High Court in London. There this particular battle against the Council was lost, judgment being given against the Vicar and Churchwardens with costs.

CHAPTER TEN

LOCAL GOVERNMENT AND POLITICS

Manorial Courts

Manorial Courts operated under various different names. Those in East Lincolnshire were generally called the 'Court Leet, View of Frankpledge and Court Baron'. The Courts Leet, Courts Baron and so on had had different origins but they had, for centuries at least, been held as one and the same Court for each Manor with a single jurisdiction, whether criminal, manorial or civil. In the Middle Ages, what local government there was, the Manorial Courts provided.

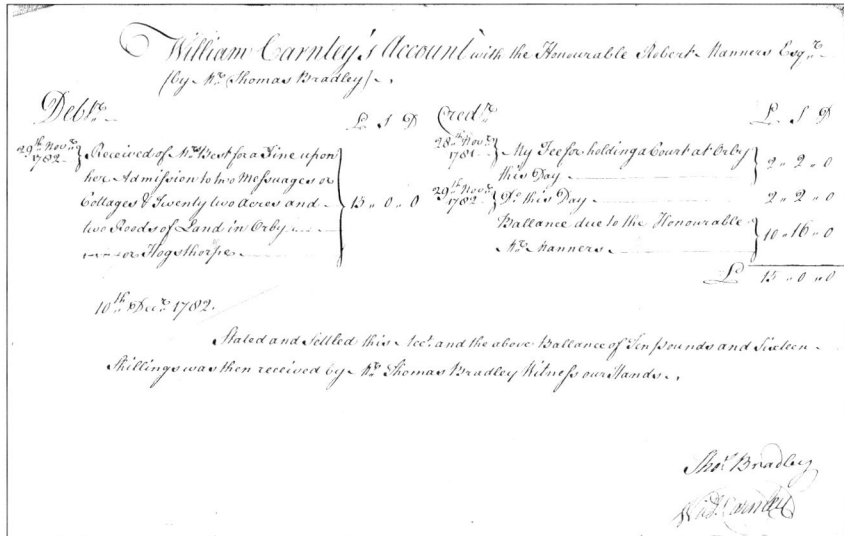

80. William Carnley's account to the Manners Estate for the holding of Orby Manorial Court in 1781-82

Successive Alford solicitors held numerous local Court Stewardships over the years. The most important were those of the Courts at Alford and at the village of Orby near Skegness. One of the main purposes of the

Manorial Court was to view the Frankpledges, that is the mutual pledges of good behaviour the inhabitants owed each other, and each Court had its bye-laws setting out what the duties of the inhabitants were. The bye-laws covered such matters as checking of weights and measures, the supervision of brewers and publicans and the remedying of insanitary nuisances. Examples of fines or 'amercements' imposed at Alford in the years around 1800 are 'for a cart standing on the highway 1s 0d' 'for throwing stink pots upon the highway next to Hanby Chapel 1s 0d' and 'for Pigges in the Church yard ten times 5s 0d'.

The spirit of the Court Leet was very democratic. The poorest inhabitant could threaten the grandest to 'present' him at the Leet. Titus Bourne and William Carnley themselves were presented more than once for minor matters and so occasionally was even the Lord or Lady of the Manor.

A further important part of the Court Leet's business was the management of the common fields. The Court discussed and decided how the fields were to be cultivated and failures to observe its agricultural regulations incurred fines. When William Carnley was first appointed to his stewardships, the Manorial Court still had also the civil jurisdiction of the old Court Baron to settle claims between the inhabitants and local attorneys appeared before the Court on behalf of litigants. But this jurisdiction ceased to have relevance with the establishment of the Alford Court of Requests in 1780.

A most important function of the Manorial Court which continued well into the twentieth century was the maintenance of records of changes of ownership of copyhold (as opposed to freehold) land, copyholders holding their land from the Lord of the Manor with the Court acting as a kind of Land Registry for the Lord. Alford itself was not an area with copyhold titles but Orby very much was. And there at Orby, in the early days at least, Stewards and copyhold tenants were involved in the kind of battle of wits for which the Courts were famous all over the country. John Rowell, for example, writing to William Hardy on behalf of a lady copyholder in 1683 had several arguments as to why her rent (or 'fine') should only be a modest one, first stressing market values and the fact that the lady was a widow with many small children. And he ended powerfully 'whopeing you will use her kindily for my sake and more ispetially because she is a hansum women, for you allwayes pretened to me you had a great kindnesse for hansum women, theirefoor I desire that I may see it nowe'.

The Vestry and the Urban District Council

Until the time of Queen Elizabeth I, local government was in the hands of the gentry and clergy of the area, whether through the Manorial Courts or in their acting as Justices of the Peace. But Queen Elizabeth gave ecclesiastical parishes responsibility for local civil affairs. This was exercised through the Vestry meetings convened by the Churchwardens. The Vestry appointed part-time amateur parish officers, such as the parish surveyor, and it also levied rates. All ratepayers were entitled to attend Vestry meetings which in consequence were often held in local public houses. But by the middle of the nineteenth century the Vestry system was getting out of date and Richard Jefferies, writing in 1875, called the Vestry 'extremely limited in authority, unpopular, and without any cohesion.'

Extracts from the Bye-Laws of the Alford Local Board 1867

60 (The Surveyor) shall report to the Local Board where any house is used or intended to be used as a factory or building in which persons of both sexes and above 20 in number are employed or intended to be employed... in order that the Local Board may be enabled to require the Owner or Occupier construct a sufficient number of waterclosets and privies for the separate use of each sex.

85 (The Inspector of Nuisances) shall from time to time inspect the public Gas posts and lamps throughout the District and report the state and condition thereof to the Board and generally see that the lamps are lighted during the prescribed hours and report any deficiency either as to the number of the hours or the quality of the Gas.

86 He shall see that shop blinds are in all cases not less than 8 feet above the level of the footpath.

91 He shall under the direction of the Local Board employ a sufficient number of Scavengers for the sweeping, cleansing and watering the streets and for the removing all dust ashes rubbish and filfth therefrom...

122 Every building to be erected and used as a Dwelling House shall have in the rear or at the side thereof an open space exclusively belonging thereto to the extent at least of 150 square feet free from any erection thereon above the level of the ground. And the distance across such open space between every such building shall be two stories in height... 15 feet; if more than three stories 25 feet.

169 Every Occupier of premises shall cause all snow to be removed from the footways adjoining the premises occupied by him...

171 No night soil sewage or other contents of any cesspit nor any other noxious or offensive matter shall be conveyed through any Street or Thoroughfare within the District except within such hours as may be from time to time fixed by the Local Board...

175 Every Occupier of premises within the District shall keep clean and free from filth the footway and pavements adjoining the premises occupied by him.

---

81. Local Board of Health bye-laws

Meanwhile, however, health scares prompted by increased populations, overloaded sewerage systems and industrial pollution had resulted in extensive new sanitary legislation. Under this, application could be made to the General Board of Health in London for it to authorise the setting up of a Local Board with powers to deal with such matters as sewerage, rubbish disposal and regulation of slaughterhouses. Following a public meeting in 1866, Frederick Rhodes successfully applied to London for Alford to have its own Local Board and he and fellow-solicitor L.J. Brackenbury were appointed the Board's joint-clerks. Almost immediately thereafter the Board obtained expert advice from London as to the modernisation of Alford's drainage system which had been blamed for recent cases of 'malignant fever'. And the new Board's bye-laws contained strict new public health provisions, for example against the depositing of rubbish or litter in the streets. But a counter-petition sent to London had already reflected the opposition of many of the town's smaller ratepayers to there being a Board and afterwards widespread discontent manifested itself in a challenge to the Board's continued existence on procedural grounds. 'Party feeling ran very high' in the town but a Court hearing at Spilsby eventually ruled in favour of the Board.

A thorough reform of countryside local government in 1894 removed all the remaining civil powers of the old Vestries. Urban and Rural District Councils were established instead of the former sanitary authorities and those towns such as Alford which had had a Local Board got their own U.D.C., whereas neighbouring Spilsby, which had had no Local Board, was thrown with its surrounding villages into a Rural District Council.

Perhaps perceiving the new Urban District Council as a threat to his own powerful influence in the town, S.B. Carnley fought battles with it in its early days on a number of fronts. Temporary peace was made when his junior partner, Geoffrey Staniland, had become Clerk to the Council and, eventually after the 1939-45 War, John Tinn, as the then Clerk, set up the U.D.C.'s office in the back rooms of his own premises.

Mid-Nineteenth Century Parliamentary Politics

Until 1832 Parliamentary seats were generally rotten boroughs bought or inherited rather than contested. The whole of Lincolnshire was one two-member parliamentary constituency and any necessary voting by the very small electorate took place at Lincoln only. The 1832 Reform Act firmly established the principle of representation. It did not at all however

FREEHOLD
HOUSES & GARDENS
ALFORD, LINCOLNSHIRE.
TO BE
Sold by Auction,
BY
Mr. W. Morton,
AT THE WIND-MILL INN, IN ALFORD
On TUESDAY, the 21st day of APRIL, instant,
AT FIVE O'CLOCK IN THE AFTERNOON,
SUBJECT TO SUCH CONDITIONS AS WILL BE THEN AND THERE PRODUCED;

A FREEHOLD
ESTATE

Situate in the West Street of Alford aforesaid, either altogether or in Lots as under, Viz.

Lot 1. Two Tenements or Dwelling Houses, one occupied by John Shaw, and the other by Reuben Keightley, together with a parcel of Rich Garden Ground adjoining, containing 1140 square yards or thereabouts.

Lot 2. Four Tenements or Dwelling Houses in the respective occupations of John Broomfield, and others, and a parcel of Rich Garden Ground adjoining, containing 2255 square yards or thereabouts.

Lot 3. A Messuage or Dwelling House in the occupation of Mr. Dennis, Gardener and Seedsman, and the two Tenements, Buildings, and parcel of Rich Garden Ground adjoining, containing 826 square yards or thereabouts.

Each Lot will confer a good Vote for Members of Parliament, to serve for the Division of Lindsey, and the Purchasers may be accommodated with half of the Purchase Money of each Lot, on Security thereof.

Further Information may be obtained on application either to Mr. JULIAN, of Woodthorpe; to Mr. JOSEPH HILL, of Trusthorpe; (the Trustees for Sale of the Property,) or at the Offices here, (where a Plan of the Estate may be seen,) or at Spilsby on a Monday of

Messrs. Bourne & Son,
ALFORD, 3RD APRIL, 1835.   *SOLICITORS.*

W. T. NORTH, PRINTER, &c. ALFORD.

82. Purchasers at this 1835 Auction Sale would be entitled to vote for MPs following the widening of the franchise under the 1832 Reform Act

envisage there being universal suffrage but a franchise based on property qualifications to extend the vote to approximately one in five adult males over the country.

After 1832 voters in a new two-member North Lincolnshire constituency could poll at their nearest market town where a special electoral court, presided over by a barrister, kept an electoral register of those entitled to vote. The political parties employed Principal Legal Agents in every constituency and District solicitor-agents in each polling district to ensure the electoral Courts had admitted their supporters to the register. One of the new polling districts was centred at Alford.

Well-established country solicitors such as Titus Bourne often regarded political work simply as business and were prepared to act for either party without regard to their own political opinions or the political influence of

82. R.A. Christopher, MP for North Lincolnshire 1837-57 and the owner of several very large Lincolnshire estates

their clients. Alford at the time was a Liberal stronghold. Titus Bourne was also himself personally a Liberal but he found no difficulty in acting as district agent for the Conservative constituency member, R.A. Christopher. District political agents like Titus Bourne were paid a modest annual retainer though higher fees could be charged in an election year.

For Principal Agents, who had the whole direction of their candidate's election campaign and synchronised the work of the sub-agents in the districts, political work was very important business. Thomas Rhodes, Frederick's father, was Principal Agent for Christopher's Liberal rival, the other North Lincolnshire MP, Sir Montague Cholmeley. And his bill for running Cholmeley's 1852 election campaign was £600.

In the event, the 1832 reforms were only a step on the way to universal suffrage. And with the 1867 Reform Act further extending the franchise and the 1872 Ballot Act introducing secret voting, the need for the political parties to have specialist local legal agents disappeared.

Cemeteries and The Burial Board

Traditionally burials took place in the graveyards adjoining parish churches without too much concern about successive generations being buried on top of each other. But the nineteenth century population explosion caused congestion especially in urban churchyards. And the Victorians' concerns about public health and the increasing demand for permanent stone graveyard memorials led to legislation allowing parish vestries to set up Burial Boards with authority to close the old churchyards and locate new cemeteries in their place.

It was to be some years before there was a Burial Board in Alford but the new Act was the incentive for the church authorities themselves to have the church graveyard closed in 1855 and to replace it with a new cemetery in South Street. However, the church's new cemetery only provided a short respite and in 1879 the Vicar was reporting to a Vestry meeting that 'the present state of the Parish Churchyard was not what Christian people would wish God's acre to be'.

Early in 1880 a Burial Board was formally set up and land purchased in Farlesthorpe Road for a new cemetery with mortuary chapel which was officially opened in 1883. S.B. Carnley was Clerk and Registrar to the Board from 1892. His duties involved the allocation of grave spaces,

ALFORD BURIAL COMMITTEE.

To be Sold by Auction, by

E. H. YOUNG

On the recently-purchased field adjoining the Cemetery,

On Thursday, the 11th day of January, 1923,

AT 2.30 P.M.,

SEVERAL FAGGOTS

AND

FIREWOOD

The Faggots will be sold in bundles of ten.

The purchase money is to be paid to the Auctioneer immediately after the sale, and the lots purchased removed without delay.

S. B. CARNLEY,

5th JANUARY, 1923.

CLERK.

Brittan Wakelin Printer Alford

84. Early in the last century, expensive printing costs could be justified for advertising the sale of firewood

the collection of fees, the approval of monuments and gravestones, the employment of cemetery workmen and also the selling of grass crops and firewood gathered from the cemetery grounds.

For its first few years, the Alford Burial Board was elected by the Vestry but, as a result of the local government upheaval of 1894, it came under the wing of the newly-created Alford Urban District Council as simply the Burial Committee of the Council. Carnley, having been from the very first in a state of continuous feud with the leading lights among the new Councillors, wrote up to the Local Government Board in London to check what his powers and position in relation to what he called the new 'Parish Council' would be and, upon being assured that he would act as Clerk of the Council when they proceeded under the Burial Acts, he asserted his independence throughout his reign as Clerk by having meetings of the Burial Committee taking place not at the Council's office but at his own.

On Carnley's death in 1947 John Tinn succeeded him as Burial Committee Clerk and Registrar and, although in 1965 Alford Urban District Council decided to discontinue the Burial Committee as an independent entity, Mr. Tinn's appointment as Burial Registrar continued until the local council was itself abolished.

Latter-day Manorial Courts

By the beginning of the nineteenth century Manorial Courts in many parts of the country had long ago ceased to exist but those at both Alford and Orby were still very much alive.

Meetings of the Alford Court, held annually in October, were from time immemorial at the Windmill Hotel and those at Orby at the Red Lion. Good dinners, heavily subsidised by the Lord of the Manor, were always supplied. The Steward presided over the Court as the Lord of the Manor's representative but he had to be a man 'indifferent between the Law and the Lord' and in the balance of authority the Court's Jurors had the overriding power. The Carnleys and Bournes were certainly well on top of their Stewardships and some efficient office notes, probably prepared by Henry Bourne, survive, setting out fully a model of the Steward's Charge to be read at the Alford Court and the detailed Court procedure the Steward was to follow.

The Alford Manorial Court fought strong rearguard actions to try to preserve its authority against the national developments which were increasingly restricting its powers. In 1844 the Bournes obtained Counsel's Opinion to reassure them that the Court's bye-Laws were in general still enforceable and that, in particular, the Court's Jurors could carry on with their custom

SIDNEY SUTTON,

Wind Mill

Family, Hotel, Commercial Gin, and

AND POSTING HOUSE,

ALFORD.

J.C.Greaves & Son fc

	Miles		Miles	Birmingham.
Spilsby	9	Horncastle	16	
Louth	4	Skegness	16	

		£	s	d
22 Dinners — 2/-		2	4	0
14 Bottles Wine 5/-	3	10	—	0
1 Cigars — 3/-		3	—	
Ham 2/6 —		2	6	
1 Pt Ale for Mill —			6	
		6	—	0
Dr Mr Christopher	3	—	0	0
Lewis	3	—	0	0
	—	5	—	0
	3	—	5	0

85. At Manorial Courts, as Reginald Hine described it from his experience at Hitchin, "eating and drinking were the business, and later on the burden of the day" as this early 19th century Alford Manorial Court entertainment account shows.

of weighing butter and testing weights and measures in Alford's Market Places regularly each year. So, in the face of the modern world, the Court continued in its old way, formally presenting and amercing the Great Northern Railway Company, for instance, in 1857, for the use of six weights which were defective in terms of Alford's own local standards.

The power of regulating weights and measures was one which the Manorial Court jealously guarded. Sharp conflict arose in 1859 when, as a result of new statutory provisions, the County Police Superintendent gave formal notice that he would be attending at Alford to check the weights. A counter-notice was issued declaring that no person needed to submit to the Police Superintendent's inspections as these conflicted with the powers of the Court Leet. Hardly any of Alford's tradesmen did cooperate with the Superintendent and Rhodes sought Counsel's Opinion as to whether the Superintendent himself might be presented to the Manor Court and amerced for his conduct. But Counsel declared that the Court no longer had the jurisdiction it claimed and the Superintendent had to have his own way.

After the death of Titus Bourne, coinciding with the reverse on the weights and measures issue, Rhodes came to the conclusion that the powers and duties of the Manorial Courts had really by then been vested by statute in other bodies and that the expense of holding further Courts was no longer justified. Some perfunctory meetings continued to be held and, of course, regular meetings of the Orby Court continued to be necessary to deal with transfers of properties with copyhold title, not abolished until 1925.

Sidney Carnley himself always contended that it would have been preferable to continue to hold the Alford Court periodically, even with meetings at some distance apart. But at the last one, which was eventually held in 1874, shortly after he had joined Rhodes as an articled clerk, it was firmly asserted and placed on record that the Lord of the Manor retained for the future his right to Tolls for all livestock or goods sold or stalls erected in any of Alford's Market Places.

LINCOLNSHIRE
CONSTABULARY

NOTICE IS HEREBY GIVEN that Mr. **JAMES STRUGNELL**, Superintendent of County Police, Lincoln, having been appointed **INSPECTOR** of **WEIGHTS** and **MEASURES** for the Petty Sessional Divisions of Alford and Spilsby; will attend at the undermentioned places on the days and dates specified below, for the purpose of comparing and stamping, if found correct, all such Measures as shall be brought to him for that purpose, in the manner and form prescribed by the Act 5 and 6, William IV, cap. 63.

DISTRICT.	TOWNS.	PLACE OF ATTENDANCE.	DAY AND DATE.
	SPILSBY	Town-hall	Tuesday, 15th & 22nd Feb., 1859.
No. 1.	ALFORD	Police Station	Wednesday, 16th & 23rd ,, ,,
	BURGH	Bell Inn	Friday, 25th ,, ,,
	WAINFLEET	Angel Inn	Tuesday. 1st March ,,

The Superintendent will also at any time Compare and Stamp Weights and Measures brought for that purpose to the County Police Station at ~~Lincoln~~, provided that other duties do not prevent his so doing. *Spilsby*

All persons using Weights and Measures for the sale of any article are requested to take notice, that visits for the purpose of examining and testing the Weights and Measures in use will commence forthwith.

The following Extract from the Act 5 and 6, Wm. IV, cap. 63, is published for general information.

"And every person who shall use any Weight or Measure other than those authorised by this Act, or "some aliquot part thereof, as hereinbefore described, or which has not been so stamped as aforesaid, or "which shall be found light, or otherwise unjust, shall, on conviction, forfeit a sum not exceeding FIVE "POUNDS, and any contract, bargain, or sale, made by such Weights or Measures, shall be wholly null "and void, and every such light or unjust Weight and Measure so used, shall on being discovered by any "Inspector, so appointed as aforesaid, be seized, and on conviction of the person using or possessing the "same, shall be forfeited."

Chief Constable's Office, Lincoln, Feb. 4th, 1859.

Edward R. Cousans, Printer, ⸺ ⸺ ⸺, ⸺⸺⸺⸺

86. In 1859 the recently-established County Police, announcing in this notice their intention to inspect and regulate local weights and measures…

MANORS

OF

WELL, ALFORD,

AND

MAWTHORPE.

WHEREAS the Superintendent of Police at ALFORD has lately caused a Notice to be given to the Tradesmen within these Manors, requiring them to produce their Weights and Measures at the Police Office in Alford, on Wednesday the 16th of February, instant, in order that the same may be tested and stamped, or in default they will be liable to have them seized, besides incurring certain penalties.

NOTICE IS HEREBY GIVEN,

That no person within these Manors is compelable to produce his or her Weights or Measures to the Superintendent of Police in Alford or elsewhere, for any purpose whatsoever,---the Act of 5 & 6, Will. IV, relating to Weights and Measures, (an Extract from which is given below), *expressly reserving to Leet Juries the authority which they possessed of examining and regulating Weights, Balances, and Measures within their Jurisdictions.*

BY ORDER,

THOMAS BRADLEY,

FOREMAN OF THE LEET JURY FOR THE ABOVE MANORS.

ALFORD, 15th FEBRUARY, 1859.

Extract from Act 5 and 6 William IV, cap. 63.

" Provided always, and be it enacted, that nothing in this Act contained shall extend or be construed to extend to
" supersede, limit, take away, lessen, or prevent the authority which any person or persons, bodies politic or corporate,
" or any person appointed at any Court Leet for any Hundred or Manor, or any Jury or Ward Inquest, may have or
" possess for the examining, regulating, seizing, breaking, or destroying any Weights, Balances, or Measures within their
" respective Jurisdictions, or the power given by any Act or Acts now in force to Justices or other authorities, to appoint
" Examiners for the Inspection of Weights and Measures."—See. 45.

MOUNTAIN AND MARSHALL, PRINTERS, MARKET-PLACE. ALFORD

87. …found their authority to do so immediately contested in a counter-notice issued by the Manorial Court.

The Alford Fair

In 1896 a bitter dispute arose in the town about the fixing of the day for the Alford Autumn Fair. Carnley, as Steward of the Manor of Alford with Well, acted for the Lady of the Manor, Mrs Hamilton Ogilvy, and claimed for her the sole right to hold markets and fairs in the town and to appoint the landlord of the Windmill Hotel as collector of the market tolls. Her claim was however disputed by the recently established Alford Urban District Council, and court action was eventually required to settle the position.

ALFORD NOVEMBER FAIR.
SATURDAY, 7th NOVEMBER, 1896.

NOTICE is hereby given, that the above FAIR will be held on the date above named, upon the Lands provided by the Lessee of the Tolls under the Lady of the Manor of Alford

And Notice is hereby also given, that after the appearance of this advertisement any persons or bodies holding or attempting to hold or advertising the holding of any Fair within the precincts of the Manor of Alford-with-Well on any other date or in any other place than those indicated above will be treated as infringing the rights of the Lady of the above Manor and her Lessees.

Dated this Nineteenth day of October, 1896.

JOHN & FREDERIC HIGGINS, { Agents for MARY GEORGIANA CONSTANCE CHRISTOPHER NISBET HAMILTON OGILVY Lady of the above Manor.

HEWITT, BROS., LIMITED,
CHARLES BIRKETT, { Lessees of the above Tolls.

S. B. CARNLEY, { Steward of the above Manor.

ALFORD URBAN DISTRICT COUNCIL.
NOVEMBER FAIR.

Notice is hereby given, that ALFORD NOVEMBER FAIR will be held on Monday the 9th day of November, 1896.—By order.   J. E. H. SERGEANT, Clerk.

---

88. The competing notices advertising the 1896 Alford November Fair appeared next to each other in the Stamford Mercury

The Alford Fair was held twice a year, on Whit Tuesday and 8th November, and the practice had always been that when the November date fell on a

Sunday the Lady of the Manor fixed an alternative date and advertised it accordingly. In 1896 the Agent for the Lady of the Manor, Mr J.F. Higgins, announced that, 8th November being a Sunday, Saturday 7th November was to be fixed for the Alford Fair. Matters then came to a head because the newly elected Council, according to the partisan documentation Carnley had prepared, included a radical element which decided to overturn a previous Council vote not to contest Mrs Ogilvy's rights. The Council had a counter-notice issued to the effect that the fair would be held on the Monday 9th November. Rival wall posters, handbills and press announcements then proliferated, with the Stamford Mercury carrying notices next to each other in the self-same issue, advertising the conflicting dates for the Fair.

The legal argument was intense and Carnley re-enforced his case on a more practical level by having the majority of the local auctioneers advertise that they would hold their Stock Sales on 7th November only. The town was generally upset by the confusion. But in the end, a Court Injunction bludgeoned the Council into submission and the Mercury on 11th December reported that a committee had been formed to 'wait upon the plaintiff's Solicitor to arrive at a settlement of costs'.

Unpleasant echoes of the case continued to be heard for some time. According to the Hull Daily Mail on 10th February 1897, the landlord of the Windmill claimed toll from an itinerant Methodist preacher in the Market Place, 'much to the amazement of the Evangelist', and after 'a good Samaritan came up and paid the amount asked.....a crowd gathered round the lessee of tolls and booed and hissed him'.

Manorial Rights to Market Tolls

After the reassertion in 1874 of the Lord of the Manor's rights to receive live and dead tolls, they remained unchallenged for some years. And the 1920s legislation abolishing copyhold tenure had left in place vestigial manorial rights as to the holding of Markets and Fairs.

'Live tolls' (i.e. on sales of livestock), originally exacted on sales of cattle in the South Market Place, were leased by the Manor to the Alford Cattle Market Company on its setting up the East Street Cattle Market in 1912. However, a poultry auction with market stalls for sale of general goods continued to be held in the Market Places each Tuesday and tolls for these ('dead tolls') continued to be paid to the Manor's Lessees of Tolls. Eventually a row blew up about the collection of tolls for the use of the areas outside shops on the east side of the South Market Place. One or two of the shopkeepers objected to paying tolls to be able to expose goods outside their shops and one Tuesday in March 1923 blocked off the area against the Lessee of Tolls. Once again, Chancery proceedings were used to re-establish the Manorial rights.

And so the last vestige of Alford's Manorial rights remained for Carnley's lifetime and he continued to advertise the annual Alford Fair on behalf of the Lord of the Manor right to the end. It was only after his death that the Alford Urban District Council in 1949 at last took a transfer of the manorial rights to the market tolls.

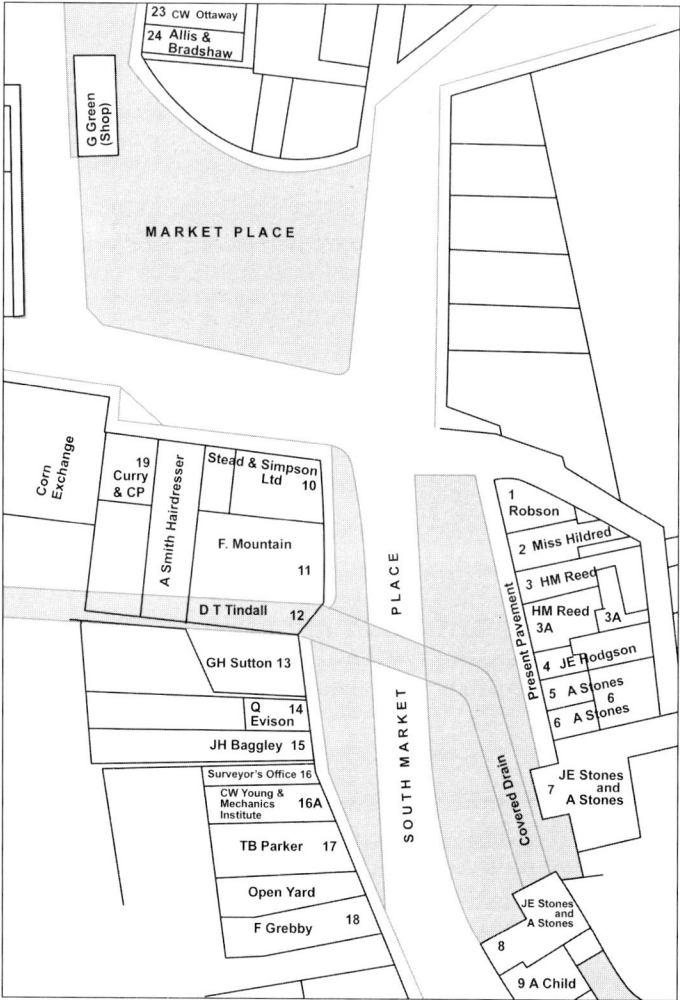

89. Areas of central Alford claimed for the Manor in 1926 as "Lord's Waste" for the collection of Market Tolls

ALFORD WINTER FAIR

The Manor of **WELL,**
ALFORD, and
MAWTHORPE.

NOTICE IS HEREBY GIVEN

that in pursuance of the powers vested in

the Lord of the above Manor
THE ALFORD WINTER FAIR

will be held on

SATURDAY, 7TH NOV. 1942

In consequence of the 8th day of November,
1942 falling upon Sunday.

Dated this 3rd Day of October, 1942

S. B. CARNLEY,

Steward of the Manor.

C. A. DUNN, Printer, Market Place, ALFORD.

90. S.B. Carnley continued to assert the Manorial Rights up to his death in 1947

119

EPILOGUE

A fter the death of S.B. Carnley in 1947, John Tinn ran his practice for many years with Robert Hornby as its anchorman. And for quite some time the two of them continued to hold most of the public offices at the centre of town life. Indeed these official duties claimed more of John Tinn's time than did his legal work. The Alford Urban District Council itself was for some time run from his firm's High Street premises with himself as Clerk. He was also at one time or another Clerk to the Alford Drainage Board, Clerk to the local Commissioners of Taxes and Clerk to the Justices not only at Alford (where Sam Baggley for many years ran the Court Office from the High Street premises) but also at the neighbouring Magistrates Courts at Spilsby, Skegness and Louth. And Robert Hornby and he were successive Clerks to the Grammar School and were also successively local Agents of the Halifax Building Society. In the postwar World, however, the threat was not so much, as Bourne, Rhodes and Carnley had seen it, from outside interference with the traditional institutions managing Alford's affairs. It was more, with such closures as those of the Court, local Council and drainage board offices, the cattle market and corn exchange and the railway station, to the very existence of administrative and commercial institutions in the little country town.

91. Robert Hornby

APPENDIX 1

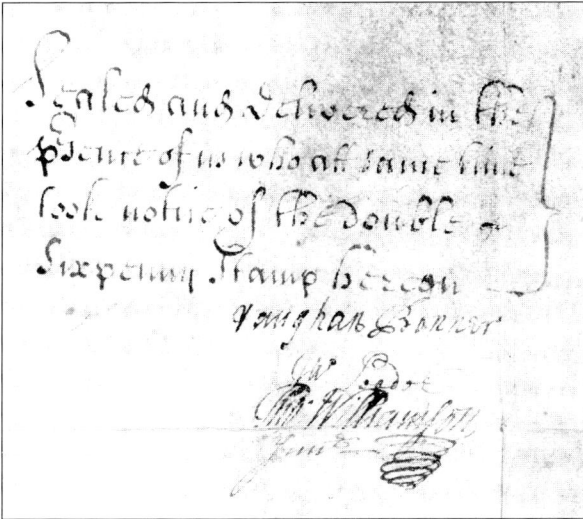

92. In this Indenture of 1712 the Alford Solicitor Vaughan Bonner was a witness to the disposal of their Alford property by the successors of William Willerton who had practised there in the mid-seventeenth century. Stamp duties had only been introduced for the first time in England as recently as 1694 but were immediately seen to be successful money-raisers and have been in force ever since. As can be seen, attesting witnesses were required to check the stamping of early deeds.

APPENDIX 2

93. The two photographs on this page were taken by the well-known local photographer Edward Nainby, who also took many of the other old photographs reproduced in this book. In the one of S.B. Carnley's office staff above, taken in about 1896, smoking equipment is very much in evidence.

94. This photograph was taken outside Nainby's premises of the men who posed inside against a backcloth on the same day in 1897 (illustration no 45). In the front row, J.E. Bickerton and E.T. Williams, first and second left, were long-time Alford residents, while J.E. Richards, on the right, went on to have a distinguished career as Town Clerk of Nottingham.

BIBLIOGRAPHY

T.W. Beastall: Agricultural Revolution in Lincolnshire (1978)

Geoffrey Best: Mid-Victorian Britain 1851-75 (1985)

M. Birks: Gentlemen of the Law (1960)

J. Boyes and R. Russell: The Canals of Eastern England (1977)

C. Brears: Lincolnshire in the Seventeenth and Eighteenth Centuries (1940)

J.N. Clarke: Education in a Market Town - Horncastle (1976)

P.G.M. Dickson: The Sun Insurance Office 1710 - 1960

George Dow: Alford & Sutton Tramway (1984)

R.C. Dudding: History of Alford with Rigsby (1930)

J.R. Elkington: Alford Drainage Board - 50 years (1987)

Richard Gurnham: Georgian Spilsby (1989)

A.S. Hackett: Queen Elizabeth's Grammar School Alford (1966)

D.H. Hamilton: The Diaries of George Langton 1647 - 1727 (1998)

R.L. Hine: Confessions of an Uncommon Attorney (1945)

Bibliography

Clive Holmes:	Seventeenth Century Lincolnshire (1980)
N.J. Hone:	The Manor and Manorial Records (1906)
H. Kirk:	Portrait of a Profession (1976)
A.J. Ludlam:	The East Lincolnshire Railway (1991)
W.O. Massingberd:	History of Ormsby
R.E. Megarry:	Miscellany-at-Law (1955)
R.E. Megarry:	A Second Miscellany-at-Law (1973)
G.E. Mingay:	Rural Life in Victorian England (1977)
P. Montague - Smith:	The Bournes of Dalby and Partney in Lincolnshire Life 20/01/28
J. Obelkevich:	Religion and Rural Society in South Lindsey 1825-75 (1976)
R.J. Olney:	Rural Society and Government in 19th Century Lincolnshire (1979)
R.J. Olney:	Lincolnshire Politics 1832-85 (1973)
Charles K. Rawding:	The Lincolnshire Wolds in the Nineteenth Century (2001)
R. Robson:	The Attorney in Eighteenth Century England (1959)
J.G. Ruddock and R.E. Pearson:	The Railway History of Lincoln (1974)
Albert J. Schmidt:	Articles in Lincolnshire History and Archaeology Journal Vol 32 1997 and Vol 37 2002

Christopher Sturman: Mrs Lloyd's recollections of Tennyson in
                        the 1830s Lincolnshire History and
                        Archaeology Journal Vol 28 1993

D. Sugarman: A Brief History of the Law Society (1995)

Scriven: Copyholds (1896)

Charles Tennyson
and Hope Dyson: The Tennysons: Background to Genius (1974)

G.M. Trevelyan: English Social History (1944)

W. White: 1856 Directory of Lincolnshire

G.B. Wood: Alford - The Industrial Archaeology

G.N. Wright: Turnpike Roads (1991)

Neil R. Wright: Lincolnshire Towns and Industry
                        1700 - 1914 (1982)

ACKNOWLEDGEMENTS
AS TO ILLUSTRATIONS

Reproduction of illustrations nos 16, 17 and 18 from the Tennyson Research Centre and of no 20 from the Local Studies Collection, Lincoln Central Library, is by courtesy of Lincolnshire County Council and illustration nos 22, 38, 39, 64 and 69 from the Local History Photograph Collection at Grimsby Central Library are reproduced by courtesy of North East Lincolnshire Council.

The portrait of Lucy, the eighteenth century Duchess of Rutland, is reproduced by kind permission of the present Duke and that of R.A. Christopher (R.A. Dundas), held by the Scottish National Portrait Gallery, by kind permission of the owners.

Pictures for illustrations have also kindly been provided by Mrs Suzette Cooke (nos 93 and 94), Miss Diana Loy (no 12), Mrs Joan Morris (no 29), Mr Tom Porter (nos 61, 72 and 77) and Mr Andrew Willoughby (no 92).

The cartouche of Dalby Hall was prepared by John Brookes of Withern and David Pleming of The Centrepiece, Spilsby, has helped with photography and the preparation of illustration for printing.

INDEX

(Titus Bourne, F.J. Rhodes and S.B. Carnley are not separately noticed, being referred to frequently throughout)

Index